BEYOND PSYCHOLOGY

BEYOND PSYCHOLOGY
The Potential of Conscious Thinking

NONA COXHEAD

Mandala
An Imprint of HarperCollins*Publishers*

Mandala
An Imprint
of HarperCollins*Publishers*
77-85 Fulham Palace Road,
Hammersmith, London W6 8JB

Published by Mandala 1991
1   3   5   7   9   10   8   6   4   2

A CIP catalogue record for this book
is available from the British Library

ISBN 1-85274 068 X

Printed in Great Britain by
Woolnough Bookbinding Limited,
Irthlingborough, Northamptonshire
Typesetting by MJL Limited,
Hitchin, Hertfordshire

CONTENTS

DEDICATION

To the memory of R.C.B. — teacher without equal.

ACKNOWLEDGEMENTS

The author acknowledges with gratitude all those original thinkers quoted in her book, each of whom are credited and identified in the text or bibliography.

PREFACE

The inspiration to write this book came as the result of a conviction that had gathered force in steps and stages of my personal search into the meaning of human existence, and which, finally, impelled me towards a very large, very optimistic claim.

The claim, admittedly only verifiable by those who test it, was formed in answer to looming, age-old philosophical questions: Is there anything we can do about our own individual lives, other than cope, manage, adapt, pray, survive in the only ways available to us? Can we have any real *say* in our own destinies? Can we, as seemingly separate entities in a vast universal scheme that remains largely mysterious and unknowable to us, shape the events and conditions of our personal experience? Can we gain control, take charge, of that which appears to be beyond our human jurisdiction?

The answer to all these questions is — yes. My claim is that we not only can, but *do*, have a say. We can take charge of what happens to us. We are *not* helpless. We do have means within our power to create the good, valuable, fulfilling and meaningful lives we want, without needing to defer to any overwhelming precedents of human behaviour, belief systems, or concepts of predetermined fate.

As I now approach the daunting challenge of underpinning my thesis with the brick and mortar of persuasion, I am well aware that what I propose as the substance of my claim is no escape route, no by-pass, no magic formula, no strategy for avoiding confrontation with the realities of the human state. It is indeed far from being as easy in achievement as in intellectual grasp.

This, however, in no way diminishes the reliability and potential of a life principle that can be made to prove itself in the application not just by strong, unusual people, but by everyone, simply by choice. Whether or not it is chosen, is up to each one of us.

But first, the brick and mortar.

I would like to thank my publishers for this opportunity to present my case, to reach out with it into a world showing itself ready for change, for going 'Beyond. . .'. I would also like to thank my readers for giving it consideration in their search for more than hope and promise.

Nona Coxhead
London, 1990

INTRODUCTION

When I first thought of the title *Beyond Psychology*, I thought it not only apt and descriptive of my intention, but moderately distinctive, if not unusual. I was in for a considerable surprise. In the course of initial research, I soon discovered that the term 'beyond' was so widely used, a prefix to such a diversity of hypotheses, that its dictionary definition — 'on the farther side of' — was suddenly fraught with significance.

Here, for instance, are a few of the titles I found had preceded or co-existed with my 'inspired' choice: Beyond Ego; Beyond Einstein; Beyond the Brain; Beyond Telepathy; Beyond Feedback; Beyond Health and Normality; Beyond Freedom and Dignity; Beyond Chains of Illusion; Beyond the Pleasure Principle; Beyond Fear; Beyond Reductionism; Beyond Death — and then, in reverse in the same mode: Physics and Beyond; Quantum Physics and Beyond, and no doubt others too numerous to add.

What did this have to reveal that might be not only important but crucial to understand?

As I came to see it, it had to be an evolutionary point in the growth of human self-awareness, a stage of arrival at boundaries of assumptions that now required to be explored for newer and greater possibilities. This was both encouraging and awesome, and for a short time I considered defecting to a less demanding realm, choosing another title altogether. Something, however, urged me to persist. I still liked the original concept and it was still descriptive of my intent. I kept it.

This brings me to explain why it is psychology I have chosen to go beyond. The reason is that psychology — 'study of the mind' — is the primary focus of interest in the phenomena of human behaviour, the most widespread form of search and research, theory, experiment and application of its manifest effects in the modern Western world. What more logical place to take off from than one with such an established familiarity, and of such immense influence in the lives of so many people?

However, in case I give the impression that a scholarly presentation of psychology, as a subject, now follows, let me hasten to say that this is not the case. Countless volumes exist of comprehensive histories and textbooks of psychology considered from a multitude of perspectives and viewpoints. In no way would I attempt to enter the field of such expertise and erudition.

What I do venture to give is a generalized record of its salient aspects, its roots, the directions of its growth, and the many forms in which it proliferates in our society today.

From there, again without presuming further than a layman's grasp of the subject, I press on beyond the boundaries of psychology, and consider the laws perceived by science to run the universe, with man and without him; and then even further to explore the question of a possible interfusion of the physical and 'meta-physical', as suggested by the New Physics. After this, I forego speculation as to the significance of all these accumulated data on the phenomenon of human existence, and take up my own thesis.

I propose a *conscious* universe, in which man has direct access to self-knowledge and self-control, using the same laws to support his thought and make it manifest. I present comprehensive explanatory detail and provide an unambiguous 'how to' manual for taking charge of one's own experience, one's own 'destiny'.

The reader who is more interested in the potential of Conscious Thinking than in Psychology or New Science can go straight to Part III. However, it is preferable to read those sections also, since they lay the foundations for the principle that leads to conviction.

I hope this collection of 'do-it-yourself' methods and ideas, both practical and specific, will prove my unreserved claim that each and every member of the human race has the creative power to rule his own life — and make it good.

PART I

PSYCHOLOGY

If you want to change a person's mind, you must know how his mind was made up to begin with. And that is, after all, the central question for any science of psychology.

George A. Miller

1

ORIGINS AND
FOUNDATION

> Up until a century ago psychology was a branch of
> philosophy; the great thinkers somehow knew what
> was true and spent their days inventing clever
> arguments designed to prove it.
>
> George A. Miller

The great thinkers referred to are, of course, the philosophers of
Antiquity, of ancient Greece in particular, and most specifically
Socrates, his student Plato, and Plato's student Aristotle. Their
respective methods of inquiry and definition of the nature and
purpose of human existence still underlie and influence our current Western search for definitive answers and meanings.

A century ago, largely through the speculations and theories
of William James, the American philosopher (1842-1910), attention became focused on the possibility of psychology becoming
a science in its own right, not separate from philosophy but
branching off into a systematized process of observation. James's
background was ideal for this gradual transition: at Harvard he
had taught physiology and physiological psychology. His next
move was to psychology, at that time within the Department of
Philosophy. In 1890 his many-volumed work, *The Principles of Psychology*, which had taken 12 years to write, created a stir of new
speculation about the significance of mental life and experience,
the roles of instinct, emotion, and will. His interpretations were
not founded on any analytical method but on his own perceptions and observations during the course of his combined medical and philosophical studies.

Explaining his main premise, he wrote:

> Our natural way of thinking about these coarser emotions
> is that the mental perception of some fact excites the

mental affection called the emotion, and that this latter state of mind gives rise to the bodily expression. My theory, on the contrary, is that the bodily changes follow directly on the perception of the exciting fact, and that our feeling of the same changes as they occur is the emotion.

Common sense says, we lose our fortune, are sorry and weep; we meet a bear, are frightened and run; we are insulted by a rival; are angry and strike. The hypothesis here to be defended says that this order of sequence is incorrect, that the one mental state is not immediately induced by the other, that the bodily manifestations must first be interposed between, and that the more rational statement is that we feel sorry because we cry, angry because we strike, afraid because we tremble.

Despite ensuing controversy, these views had one enduring effect: they opened the way for further consideration of the claim of psychology to be a science (Figure 1). They did, however, leave another equally enduring question, for no matter how brilliantly conceived and enjoyably written, were they not still unverifiable opinion? The answer indicated the need for a more precise method of observation, a more direct, more controllable form of assessment — an 'experimental psychology'.

Among those moving in this direction, was Wilhelm Wundt, a German physiological psychologist at the University of Leipzig, who around 1879 opened the first psychology laboratory for the express purpose of investigating, analysing, recording and measuring images and conscious thought processes under the 'controlled' conditions required by science.

Using a method known as introspection, he devised techniques of repeated stimulus, verbal instructions, physical sounds (like the rhythmic clocking of a metronome) to measure the duration or intensity of the students' responses. Over a period of 60 years and many scholarly volumes, his tireless practice resulted in the creation of an experimental psychology that was respected, if not entirely accepted, as a science. What others had merely talked about doing, he had got on with and done. A 'new psychology' had been born of the old.

During the next two decades, however, yet another, opposing view of psychology began to establish itself with far greater impact — an influence so profound that it was to last to the present day. It took its initial focus from the attempts of current researchers to broaden the concept of mental science to include a science of

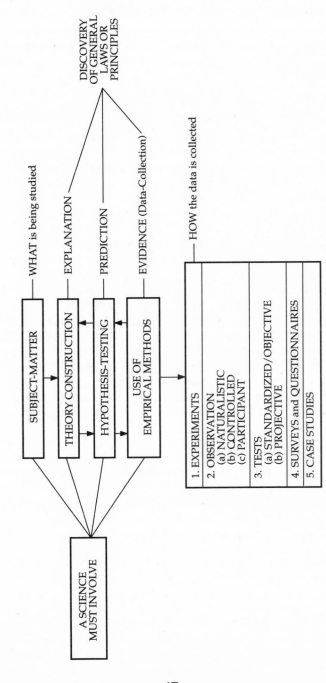

Figure 1 The major criteria of a science and the empirical methods used in psychology.

17

behaviour. In this new arena, an American psychologist, John B. Watson, led the way.

He first presented his thesis of the behaviourist system of psychology in 1908 to a seminar at the University of Chicago, and in 1919 his book, *An Introduction to Comparative Psychology* further defined his views:

> For the behaviourist, psychology is that division of Natural Science which takes human behaviour — the doings and sayings, both learned and unlearned — as its subject matter.

He proposed that it is not possible, at least at this evolutionary stage of our development, to know exactly what goes on inside another person's head; the only method of evaluation is direct observation of how a person behaves. According to their external behaviour, John B. Watson firmly upheld, their interior 'mental' processes could be considered the functions of objective mechanisms. In other words, there was no mysterious 'mind-stuff', *behaviour* was the key to all we need to know about the genus Homo sapiens.

Conditioning, learned responses to repeated stimulus and situations contrived in the laboratory, extensive studies with animals, children, and mentally 'sick' people confirmed his stand for the elimination of introspection and the whole concept of 'consciousness'. Behaviourism put its main emphasis on the biological-chemical origin of human functions; in later research, the brain itself was the primary source. To behaviourists ever since, this is the only valid claim of psychology to be a science. Whatever questions behaviourism has not yet answered, such as the nature of inspiration, love, 'God', goodness, will eventually be resolved through exhaustive research.

There were reactions against Behaviourism, particularly from the Gestalt school of psychology, Austrian in origin, which became well established in Germany and the United States in the 1930s. Its emphasis was on the interrelationship of all perceptions, that they could not be separated from the whole of which they were a part (see Figure 2).

However, a far greater challenge to the main beliefs of Behaviourism had taken root in 1900, in the theories of an Austrian doctor living in Vienna who had chosen to specialize in nervous disorders. There is hardly a thinking person in the Western world today who has not heard of Sigmund Freud, or been influenced, consciously or not, by his psychoanalytic theory of personality, in particular by his bringing into common terminology and use

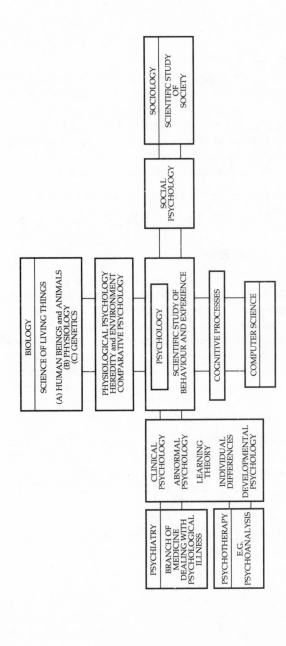

Figure 2 The relationship between psychology and other scientific disciplines.

what is called 'the unconscious'. He himself explained it this way:

> The unconscious is the true psychical reality; in its inner-
> most nature it is as much unknown to us as the reality
> of the external world, and it is as incompletely presented
> by the data of consciousness as is the external world by
> the communication of our sense organs.

The many complementary theories of his vast work together
became known as 'pschoanalysis', and to this day its immense
complexity both in application and in evaluation of the man himself continue to elicit unceasing attention and contention.

In a simplified definition of the three main components of his
overall theory, it can be said that in each one of us there exists
(psychologically, not physically) what he named as:

1. The *Id*: the deepest, unconscious part of the mind, devoted
   entirely to pleasure and driven by blind, instinctual impulses,
   which 'contains everything that is inherited, that is present
   at birth, that is laid down in the constitution — above all,
   therefore, the instincts'.

2. The *Ego*: that part of the mind that controls conscious
   experience and regulates the interactions of the person with
   the environment. Freud called it 'that part of the id which has
   been modified by the direct influence of the external world
   through the medium of conscious perception.' It can also be
   described as the 'executive' of the personality, the planning,
   reasoning and choosing aspect of ourselves, which can act as
   a buffer or mediator between the basic drives and urges of
   the instincts and the mores and requirements of the social
   order we live in.

3. The *Superego*: in our personality structure, this includes those
   prohibitions and ideals — largely unconscious — that com-
   prise its moral and judicial aspects. In Freud's own definition,
   'This new physical agency continues to carry on the functions
   which have hitherto been performed by the people in the
   external world: it observes the ego, gives it orders, judges it
   and threatens it with punishments, exactly like the parents
   whose place it has taken.'

In a very general sense, these three aspects of our psychic structure are seen as interweaving and battling within, causing an
infinite variety of havoc that translates itself into a wide variety
of physical and mental ailments, or psychoneuroses.

Freud, who in 1855 spent a year in Paris studying the effects of hypnosis on 'hysterical' patients with the famous neurologist, Jean Martin Charcot, learned much about the power of suggestion but did not feel it went deeply enough to be a permanent solution. He took another idea from a Viennese doctor, Joseph Breur, who was having some success in persuading patients to 'talk out' their problems, and finding it a much better system for uncovering the root of their problems.

Sigmund Freud adopted this method, and called it 'free association'. This was to underlie all the rest of his approach, and in listening very closely to what his patients told him, including their dreams, he began to form distinct theories, unique and controversial at the time. Terms such as 'defence mechanisms', 'repression', 'displacement', 'forgetting' (with its now famous reference to seemingly accidental lapses of memory as 'Freudian slips'), 'rationalization', 'sublimation', 'the pre-conscious' (that which is temporarily out of mind but which can be recalled), as well as the conscious and unconscious, have all infiltrated the language and science of psychology. However, one of his less acceptable theories was *infant sexuality*.

Freud firmly believed to the end that most adult neuroses (a shortened form of psychoneuroses) were due to unresolved problems from childhood, specifically related to one of the stages of sexual development. Each stage needed to be passed through fully to go on to the next; if it was not, then the entire personality of the person was fixed at that stage, thus affecting the rest of his or her behaviour and feelings throughout life. If the stages were passed in natural sequence, then the person could mature so as to manage the normal ups and downs of existence.

The sequence of these sexual stages is:

1. *Oral Stage* (0 to 1 year): pleasure from sucking, exploring objects with the mouth.

2. *Anal Stage* (1 to 3 years): pleasure transferred to the anal cavity and urinary system. Concern with expelling or retaining faeces. Parental approval or disapproval, praise, love may now depend on child's own behaviour.

3. *Phallic Stage* (3 to 5 or 6 years): focal points of pleasure now on genitals and masturbation; awareness of difference between sexes, reactions and emotional conflicts begin, with what Freud called the 'Oedipus complex' (unconscious wish to kill the father and possess the mother) in boys, and the 'Electra complex' (unconscious wish to kill the mother and possess the father, both based in mythology,) in girls.

21

4. *Latency* (5 or 6 to puberty): earlier stages are more or less repressed in favour of outward activity in learning skills or playing. Playing is very important in keeping the child's balance between id, ego and superego.
Puberty marks the crucial beginnings of

5. *The Genital Stage*: At this stage trouble may be brewing as need for the opposite sex makes its demands.

It was this emphasis on the role of sexuality which has caused Freudian analysis to be so intensely debated. While there is much undoubted truth within its concepts, it does not have the easy, self-validating acceptability of many of his other theories such as free association and dream interpretation.

Nevertheless, there is no minimizing the impact of Freud's ideas, which he went on developing after escaping to London from the Nazis in 1937, and where he died in 1939. As George A. Miller, Professor of Psychology at Princeton University, has written: 'Few men have influenced us so deeply'.

Among Freud's supporters in the formative years in Vienna were two other men destined to contribute revolutionary ideas of the human unconscious. One was Carl Gustav Jung (1875-1961), and the other Alfred Adler (1870-1937). Each was to leave a powerful influence on psychology as we know it today.

Jung became a physician at the psychiatric clinic in Zurich in 1900 and a university lecturer there in 1905. When Freud's *Interpretation of Dreams* was published in 1900, Jung became extremely interested in his ideas and the whole movement of psychoanalysis. In 1907, he met Freud and began to work closely with him, contributing several of his own concepts which won Freud's approval. In 1909 he joined Freud in a symposium at Clark University at Worcester, Massachusetts, which marked the introduction to the American public of psychoanalytic theory. Freud outlined its origin and development, and Jung spoke on 'The Association Method'. Later Jung was invited back to speak further, and accepted, but Freud, though similarly invited, declined. Jung saw the American public as open to psychoanalysis if it was freed of the weight of sexual emphasis, and this led to a break between the two men.

Subsequently, Jung's ideas became more distinctive and separate. His work led to his own system, which he called *analytical psychology*. This was an attempt at classification by psychological analysis. He divided people into two main types, 'introverts' and 'extraverts', and also introduced a far-reaching concept that he called the 'collective unconscious'.

The four major archetypes of the *Collective Unconscious* according to Jung are:

1. *The Persona* ('mask'): representing our 'facade', the outward face which both conceals the real self, and allows us to relate socially and be accepted while protecting our fragile ego.

2. *The Anima/Animus*: our unconscious 'mirror-image' of ourselves. If we are male, the anima is our unconscious female side; if we are female, the animus is our unconscious male side. We all have qualities of the opposite sex, which are expressed in different ways in different cultures, but sharing universal characteristics.

3. *The Shadow*: this represents our archetypal animal nature which, somewhat like Freud's id, must be kept in check, although too much restraint may destroy the creative impulse. So to avoid the ill effects of repression, the shadow and ego should work together in harmony.

4. *The Self*: the pivotal archetype which unifies the personality, in a stable and recognizable 'oneness'.

This theory probably divided him more than any other from Freud, in that it proposed a shared universal unconscious that is not learned but already exists in archetypes. It can be expressed as myths, and known in dreams, intuitions, and mystical insights. It is a latent reservoir for all mankind to draw on.

Jung's ideas continue to gather attention and interest in man's search for clues to himself, and his influence on current psychology is an increasing challenge to behaviourism.

Alfred Adler (1870-1937), a young Austrian medical man who joined Freud's seminar in the early part of the twentieth century, thought of himself as his junior colleague rather than a disciple, for drawn as he was to the biological and unconscious aspects of Freud's doctrine, Adler also had distinct ideas of his own which he set out to develop and expand.

The basis of these ideas is that we spend our lives compensating for feelings of inferiority established when we were helpless infants. Adults have power over infants, and in reaction to this we are all unconsciously impelled towards achieving superiority, or the will to power. There were other contributory factors, such as physical deformities; the currently assumed 'masculine' and 'feminine' weaknesses or strengths; sibling order; social and economic status of family; quality of education; pressures from parents to succeed, along an endless chain of causative, generally unconscious goals.

Some ways in which inferiority feelings are dealt with are: successful compensation, by shining out over the inferiority in some way that erases it from existence; over-compensation, in which excessive effort is made, perhaps cancelling itself in bizarre behaviour or puerile fantasies; escape from the battle altogether by deflecting energy to illness ('a chronic invalid is an incipient tyrant'), or by appearing, elaborately, not to be trying.

When Adler said, 'Every neurosis can be understood as an attempt to free oneself from a feeling of inferiority in order to gain a feeling of superiority', it was the break between his and Freud's main roads to the unconscious. Together with his rejection of the emphasis on infantile sexuality, Alfred Adler separated himself from Freud in putting greater emphasis on the social nature of man. This was to be known as 'Individual Psychology'.

The social nature of man was to occupy the concepts of later psychoanalysts, further dividing them from Freud's emphasis on the libido (energy attached specifically to the sexual instincts), in particular, Karen Horney and Erich Fromm, who, together with several others, are known as 'neo-Freudians'.

Karen Horney, as a staff member of the New York Psycho-analytic Institute, felt stifled by the orthodoxy of Freudian concepts as she moved more and more towards what she considered the social factors in neuroses. She believed that we relate much more to each other, and to the society we live in, than to the ideas of a man living in another day, with his own moral judgements, and a pioneer in treating young women suffering from 'hysteria'. While not denying the insights and value of Freud's and Adler's work, she began to stress the social forms which the insights take, the pressures which come from cultural and educational conflicts, relationships not predicated on the 'ego' or 'superego', but on conditioning and habit.

Karen Horney's work made great impact on psychology by drawing attention to the alienation and isolation that plague modern man.

Erich Fromm's main contribution to psychological theories was his challenge to Freud's 'Oedipus complex' as applicable to all cultures, and he proposed that there were cultural diversities even in the formation of character. He also emphasized, in seminars and through his many books, man's unconscious self-betrayal in order to fit in and get by, becoming a marketable commodity rather than being true to his own instincts and needs.

Following the personal and social trend of the 'neo-Freudians' (not all included here) psychology moved into even more systematic descriptions and explanations of man at the fullness of his powers as a thinking, striving, talking, 'enculturated' animal. Fields of study became divided and comparative, with so many categories as to extend beyond the possibility of a unified approach. Now there were Applied Psychology, Industrial Psychology, Psychology in Education, Medicine, Politics, Genetic Psychology, Gestalt, Group Psychology, Humanistic Psychology, and many, many others.

The next major trend was Humanistic Psychology. Founded mainly by Abraham Maslow (1908-1970), it has sought to increase the relevance of psychology to the lives of individual people. It is critical of research that trivializes human endeavour in a preoccupation with statistics, rat experiments and computer data. Abraham Maslow was an American psychologist who became known in 1958 for introducing the concept of a 'third force' in psychology (Psychoanalytic theory and Behaviourism being the first and second forces). He was more concerned with characteristics that are uniquely human, such as freedom and choice, first-hand experience of ourselves as persons.

Together with Carl Rogers (1959-00) known for his 'client-centred' form of psychotherapy, this movement has gathered impact. What Carl Rogers helped to establish was that we often hold ideas and images of ourselves that conflict with what others think of us, or the reality of the situation. For instance, we may be considered extremely successful by other people, but feel an abject failure. We may want love, but feel ourselves totally unlovable and suspect the worth of someone who loves us. It is what he called 'incongruence', and he sought to help bring to that 'congruence' a matched image, a 'positive self-regard' through talking out and thus uncovering the client's self-rejection. Much of his work was accomplished in groups of people encouraged to express their true feelings, and he was responsible for the spread and growth of what became known as 'encounter groups'.

Other forms of what Abraham Maslow called 'self-actualization' have extended the concept of 'more-to-man-than-can-be-pinned-down-and-categorized', leading toward what is called the 'consciousness revolution'.

Meanwhile, it is Intelligence Testing that prevails. Assuming intelligence to be a basic discerning faculty that can be individually rated, statistical evidence is now compiled from every possible facet of human behaviour, opinion, belief, attitude and feeling. Together with clinical predictions from both past and future as to how a person has and will react under every conceivable combination of situations and events, the Intelligence Test is accepted as the most reliable, practical tool of psychology, one which can be applied on a large, even global scale.

As George A. Miller has observed:

> Psychological dogma influences the way we discipline our children, manage our businesses, and run our marriages. Studies of abnormal behaviour modify our conception and treatment of mental illness, incompetence, perversion, criminality, and delinquency. The priest and the rabbi agree in their use of psychological techniques to guide their flocks to salvation. Novels, plays, and movies now feature psychological themes as one of their standard formulas. Psychological drugs have already changed the situation in our mental hospitals and more are yet to come. Wherever people are involved, psychology can be useful — and that is almost everywhere. Whether we like it or not, the practical application of psychology to our daily affairs is already in an advanced stage.

Included under 'psychometrics', or 'mental testing', there are also innumerable standard tests of intelligence designed to provide individual or group response that can be employed with enough certainty to justify the assumption that human beings are statistically assessable. They range from those for educational and vocational suitability and placement, aptitudes in skills, intelligence quotient (I.Q.), abilities in children of all ages, to the comparisons and differences between men and women, races and cultures, the innate and inherited, congenital and acquired.

Like consciousness, intelligence itself, except as it is demonstrated as a set of faculties, eludes precise definition. As A. Heim wrote, 'It is complex and not simple, facets are many and varied'. In other words 'true' intelligence may not lend itself to tests or testing — may not, in psychological terms, be measurable at all.

This does not prevent the infiltration of psychology further and further into daily life; sometimes reluctantly, it is given ever-increasing importance as a human reference point, as guidance, and as help in a world where confusion and trouble often seem to predominate.

2

DEVELOPMENT AND GROWTH

Today one American in three has been in psychotherapy and in 1987, 15 million of us will make roughly 120 million visits to mental health professionals — nearly twice as many visits as to internists.

Morton Hunt

According to Dorothy Rowe, a psychotherapist in Britain, this extraordinary proliferation of her profession is not an American phenomenon. In 1989 she wrote:

Psychotherapy, like television and credit cards...is big business here in the U.K. This is not so much in the private sector of health care, though the number of psychotherapists in private practice is burgeoning, but in the National Health Service and among voluntary mental health care organizations.

Psychiatrists do psychotherapy, so do psychologists, nurses, social workers and occupational therapists. If people feel that 'psychotherapy' is too pretentious a word to apply to what they do, they describe what they do as counselling, and so we have student counsellors, Samaritan counsellors, co-counsellors, bereavement counsellors, alcohol counsellors, clergy counsellors, police-women counsellors, counsellors at day centres and drop-in centres, counsellors on radio and television...Though sexual abuse of children has only recently come to be seen as a prevalent and serious problem, there are now dozens of counsellors and psychotherapists who are experts on sexual abuse, just as there are counsellors and psychother-apists who are experts on disasters like the sinking of the P & O ferry off Zeebrugge and the underground fire at King's Cross station...

Indeed there are so many counsellors and psychother-apists that I sometimes wonder if we are going to run out of people to be counselled.

In this light, psychotherapy can now be seen as the onward trend away from the strict confines of psychiatry, with its medically founded diagnoses and prescribed treatments, to that of forming relationships between the patient or client and the therapist or counsellor. The one seeking help in trouble puts himself or her-self into the hands of a trained professional who will lead the way through the painful maze to clarity and release.

The most influential psychotherapies (many come, many go in this ever-diversifying stream) are those that put value on a human relationship, are not reliant on physical or organic treatments such as drug therapies, electro-convulsive therapies (E.C.T.) or psycho-surgery on the brain (see Figure 3). They tend to fall into two categories, 'directive' and 'non-directive'.

Directive therapy does what it suggests: it directs the client into changes of behaviour that will help 'modify' or alleviate the par-ticular trouble (*Behavioural* therapy); or into thoughts and feelings which help the client to 'instruct' himself or herself by self-disclosure of negative patterns (*Cognitive* therapy); or attempt to enter the client's unique viewpoint of reality to 'get behind' the nature of the disturbance in order to give appropriate guidance (*Personal Construct* therapy). *Gestalt* therapy applies here, too, where the therapist directs clients to become aware of blocked aspects of themselves, so that they can become 'whole' expres-sions of their potential.

Non-directive therapies concentrate on the therapist and client arriving at 'insights' and revelations through mutual exploration of the distress. The therapist does not suggest so much as listen, and the therapy depends finally on his or her assumption of what is wrong. Here, an adaptive, accelerated form of *psychoanalysis* pro-vides the main foundation, but with many innovative approaches: aversions, dreads, phobias, autistic and handicapped children, compulsions and obsessions of all kinds have specialized individual modes of therapy.

The most recent developments in methods of psychotherapy are those where treatment is applied to groups rather than the individual. Some examples in this category are *Family therapy, Mar-*

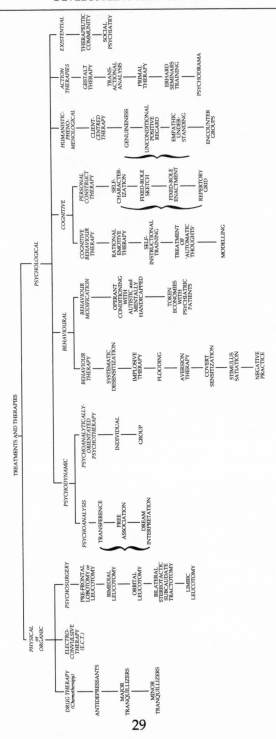

Figure 3 Major approaches to treatment and therapy.

tial Couple therapy, Feminist therapy, Eclectic therapy (where key roles in people's problems are played out within the group), and various training seminars such as *est*, using shock tactics to promote 'self-responsibility'.

From all these efforts to comprehend and deal with human needs, dilemmas and aspirations from the standpoint of psychology, the question arises as to how much has been learned, how much success has been achieved in the long, complex journey from its roots in philosophy to a vast, ever-proliferating network of therapies. After all is said and done, does psychology hold the ultimate key to human survival, growth and happiness enlightenment? There can be no question that it has contributed greatly to self-knowledge, brought much immediate relief, and will continue to offer hope and direction to Western society. But there are also some dubious aspects and disturbing shadows, both in the efficacy of its methods and the therapies themselves.

Prior to modern psychiatric treatment, people who were beyond the reach of 'normal' reasoning — who were 'mad' in the sense that they had departed from any accepted reality — were locked up as the only means of protecting society from their uncontrolled and uncontrollable behaviour. There was little if any attempt made to comprehend what lay behind their madness; there was more contempt than caring, and they were often treated as if they were a sub-human species, taunted, ridiculed, physically and mentally abused.

Gradually, the category of madness widened to include people who had merely offended the standards and norms of the prevailing society. Moralists and humanitarians began to take an interest. Those who were institutionalized were labelled and categorized, those out of step but still able to communicate were treated to experimental methods of pioneer psychology, many of which were verbally, sexually, and physically cruel.

The powers of these pioneer psychologists could fill volumes, and in the light of today is too horrific to believe, a chronicle of humiliation and degradation in which any form of abuse was sanctioned in the name of forcing a change on the patient, the change being according to the psychologist's own judgements and those of the times. Most of these imposed changes, if they did not destroy the patient, led to suicide or lifelong incarceration. If courageous and persistent victims of personal assault had not taken legal action, the world might never have known, and those involved might never have admitted their abuse of power.

Power, however, remained the lurking factor in most therapy. The psychoanalyst, in close relationship with one patient, is the norm, and is unavoidable when any troubled person seeks help from a trained professional. Willingness to do so, trust in the chosen therapist, expectation of relief and improvement, give power to the therapist in whatever form of therapy is offered. Everything, then, is dependent on the quality of the therapist and the treatment involved.

Limitations arise from the unalterable, inescapable fact that the therapist is neither perfect, nor in many instances has found any better solution to his or her own life. To maintain his authority, to convey wisdom and lead the patient into self-discovery and some form of healing insight, the therapist cannot afford to be personally vulnerable, must keep distance and the edge of superiority, must display qualities of compassion, concern, open-mindedness, friendship, and a totally non-judgemental ear into which anything and everything can be safely poured.

Further flaws are present in the very construct of such a role, for if there is any objective in therapy that stands out, it is that the therapist is there to make a change in the patient, to help him or her into another way of relating to circumstances, to cause the patient to adapt to the current expectations of society.

As Stanislav Grof has written:

> Because of the lack of precise and objective criteria, psychiatry (and psychology) is always deeply influenced by the social, cultural and political structure of the community in which it is practised. In the nineteenth century, masturbation was considered pathological, and many professionals wrote cautionary books, papers and pamphlets about its deleterious effects. Modern psychiatrists consider it harmless and endorse it as a safety valve for excessive sexual tension...
>
> In the United States, homosexuality was defined as mental illness, until 1973 when the American Psychiatric Association decided by vote that it was not. The members of the Hippie movement in the sixties were seen by traditional professionals as emotionally unstable, mentally ill, and possibly brain-damaged by drug use, while the New Age psychiatrists and psychologists considered them to be the emotionally liberated avant-garde of humanity.

If it is taken into account that every decade has its prescribed norms, then the therapist is conditioned by these, and will only consider treatment successful if the patient's attitudes have been tailored accordingly. For instance, previously an independently minded woman would have been considered successfully treated by the therapist of that era when she wanted no further part in trying to enter a 'man's world' and relaxed gracefully into her role as housewife and mother. In another time, the therapist may be helping a parent to accept that a daughter is sleeping with someone in their home as if it was a natural right.

To this effect, Nathan Hurvitz observed:

> In this way psychotherapy creates powerful support for the established order — it challenges, labels, manipulates, rejects, co-opts those who attempt to change the society.

Erving Goffman, in a similar vein, has written:

> It is understandable that a large part of psychotherapy consists of holding the sins of the patient up to him and getting him to see the error of his ways. And in a sense, I do not see how it could be otherwise.

The question left to be answered, then, is whether this inevitable deposition of power justifies the means to its ends. Does it matter that there is no other fixed criterion for the effectiveness of therapy than a kind of collusion between the patient's intense desire for good results and the therapist's techniques of persuasion that they have been achieved by a particular method? If therapy works, is how and why it does of crucial importance? Perhaps not — but when it does not seem to work, when people are only temporarily helped out of their difficulties, and then lapse back into familiar anxieties, fears or depression, or never find the 'right' therapist to trust, doubt is cast not on the therapist, but on the process itself.

Conflicting studies in recent years seem only to leave one question — is some or any form of therapy better than no therapy? There are some patients and therapists who say it is, and others who say psychotherapy is still an ambiguous, unresolvable procedure, that talking to a trusted experienced friend may generate a more honest response and possibly long-lasting benefit.

Psychology today, with all its variations of method, still appears to be outdistanced by the mysteries and unknown factors of human behaviour. It is therefore, redirecting its emphasis towards new and exploratory research, which is largely taking precedence over treatment. The research extends into every area of Western living. Relevant papers are being produced in exhaustive detail, and psychologists often pin their career goals on the hope of providing significant 'breakthroughs'. Further distanced from their patients by 'promotion' to Consultant or Principal Psychologist in charge, they are more likely to advise, inconclusively, 'more research needed'.

In the meantime, is psychology stalled, or merely marking time? New approaches may yet have the answer.

3

TREATMENTS AND THERAPIES

The secular psychotherapist is often in the role of the blind leading the half blind.

R.D. Laing

In the 1980s what is known as transpersonal psychology grew and expanded. At the far end of the spectrum from behaviourism, and an outgrowth and extension of humanistic psychology, it is described by Frances Vaughan in this way:

> Transpersonal means, literally, beyond the personal. As the study of human development beyond the ego, transpersonal psychology affirms the possibility of wholeness and self-transcendence. Transcendence is explored as manifested in and through personal experience. A transpersonal view of human relationships recognizes that we exist embedded in a web of mutually conditioned relationships with each other and with the natural environment. Any attempt to improve the human condition must therefore take global, social, and environmental issues into account.

The transpersonal therapist, therefore, is more interested in content than context — the content being determined by the client. In transpersonal therapy no limit to the range of subjective feeling is imposed, even the 'cosmic' or theistic dimension. This is a radical departure from the unwritten edict of traditional psychology to avoid all reference to any power beyond the mind-body function. As such, it illustrates the extent to which a spiritual inference has been a threat to the credibility of psychology as a 'hardnosed' science.

The language of theology was particularly to be avoided. From the time when religion was the ruling factor in Western life, when it was a matter of life or death to rebel from the Church, to the day when science took over, theological terminology has been under strict suspicion. Resistance to it has permeated Western culture. Even if people are religious by choice, they are not particularly respected for it, at least not openly. It is considered to be intellectually 'realistic' for an adult to be an atheist or agnostic. As Huston Smith says:

> Science dominates the modern mind. Through and through from promises to conclusions, the contemporary mind is science-ridden. It sways the stronger because we are unaware of its extent.

Seen from the historical perspective, this extreme position stems from the industrial revolution. Stanislav Grof writes:

> Western science has achieved astounding successes and has become a powerful force, shaping the lives of millions of people. Its materialistic and mechanistic orientation have all but replaced theology and philosophy as guiding principles of human existence and transformed to an unimaginable degree the world we live in. The technical triumphs have been so remarkable that, until recently, very few individuals questioned the absolute authority of science in determining the basic strategies of life.

It can be seen that freed from the constraint of orthodox religion, those who were psychologically ready for rebellion deserted to 'the other side' in vast numbers, churches emptied, and only that which was scientifically demonstrable was considered useful to human progress. The very concept of 'God' was retired. Suspicion, embarrassment, distaste developed for all theological terminology. To be avoided at any cost were terms such as: God, spirit, spiritual, divine, faith, religious, father, creator, soul, Lord, Saviour, holy, trinity, deity, celestial, the kingdom, and many other terms of Biblical reference.

Mention any of the above in the context of secular conversation, and the resistance, discreet or overt, is like switching off a light. To the one with 'faith', it is a total impasse; it is futile to pursue the matter. Where for the one of materialistic and mechanistic orientation theology appears to have regressed to the jargon of antiquity, superstition and ignorance, there can be no bridge of communication. Tolerance might allow an 'each to his own', or 'Sorry, I can't share your belief', but it is unlikely to go further. If there is no belief in 'God', or any creative power that cannot be biologically, chemically, physically, mathematically, subatomically, or behaviourally explained, then it is considered no more than a wistful desire for a 'big Daddy' to take care of and save mankind from its pains and inadequacies. This sharp division is intensified by the ingenuity of technical feats beyond the imagination even a few decades ago, and which will lead on apparently without limit, unless halted by ecological mistakes.

Semantically, however, of what precisely does this powerful resistance consist? Take the word 'God': What is it but a word for man's belief about himself and life? If it takes anthropomorphic shape under that name in English, there are at least a dozen others where it does not sound the same and does not conjure up quite the same image: such as Gott, in German; Dieu, in French, Dio, in Italian, Bog, in Polish; Oor, in Russian; Jumala, in Finnish; Gud, in Norwegian; Dios, in Spanish; Deus, in Portuguese (also Latin); Oeo, in Greek; Schellinkje, in Dutch; Allah, in Arabic. It is safe to say that wherever the idea of some power greater than man exists, it evokes a name to describe it. In any language it is symbolic of the principle of life, visible or invisible. It is a description of the system of cosmic life, of the whole of which man is a part.

To consider 'spirit' and 'spiritual' semantically, the dictionary defines spirit as: 'the force or principle of life that animates the body of living things; that which constitutes a person's intangible being as contrasted with his physical presence'; also: 'that animating or vital principle of persons or animals; the intelligent or immaterial part of a person; the animating or vital force of living organisms'. Spiritual: 'of spirit as opposed to matter; the nature of, relating to, the mind, the higher faculties; highly refined in thought and feeling; looking into things of the spirit'. Neither of these terms necessitates the 'either/or' of theology versus science. If 'spirit' can be taken to be the 'animating principle of body and all living things', then science, too, must call upon it for its hypotheses.

If, however, theology adapts it for its own support, the term 'divine' other than in its relation to guessing or searching or 'discovering by inspiration, magic, or prediction', becomes unequivocally theistic: by relating to, or characterizing God or deity; associated with religion or worship; devoted to God; sacred. A divine is: 'skilled in theology'. Stretched to human reference, it may mean superhuman, excellent, gifted, or beautiful.

'Faith', closely associated with faith in God, may be seen as the conviction that a principle works — that a plane or rocket will lift off, that a car will travel at high speed without its tyres bursting, that night will follow day, the sun will rise and set, the moon will stay in place, that gravitation works, and that a seed planted and watered will grow. An 'act of faith' simply means a step taken into the unknown, and does not have to be equated with trust in a deity. From the materialistic point of view, it is inseparably linked with theology. One who has 'faith' is aligned with a non-substantial reality requiring suspension of disbelief, a 'leap' over the obvious and observable facts to 'things unseen' and unknowable. The only way anything can ever be known will be through scientific corroboration, which, even if fragmented, is in its parts incontrovertible.

The term 'soul' is defined in dictionaries as 'the principle of life', 'what makes living things live', the Greek for 'alive', the Latin *animatus*, and the English 'animate'. Theologically it is associated with the Holy Ghost, that which is the divine spark or immortal aspect of human existence. As science, physical or mental, it is outside fact and reason; James Hillman puts it this way:

> Psychology does not even use the word soul (psyche): a person is referred to as a self or an ego. Both the world out there and the world in here have gone through the same process of depersonification. We have all been desouled.

With these ingrained associations, it is also of little use to point out the irony of the deeply held religious faith of, for instance, Isaac Newton in the seventeenth century whose discovery of the law of gravitation has been the model of scientific achievement for over three centuries. Similarly the great astronomer and physicist Galileo Galilei was an ardent believer, who while on trial for heresy was forced to repudiate his faith that the earth moved around the sun, while maintaining under his breath that by God's laws it did.

Today, there is no lingering trace of the heavenly roots of these original scientists and others like them; they now represent solely scientific contributions, succeeded only by more recent ones, such as Einstein's theory of relativity, or Max Planck's quantum theory.

No wonder that psychology in order to guard its secular borders has had to watch its language. But is there a price to pay for this exclusion, a delimiting factor which, at least in part, accounts for the intangible barrier which causes it to fall just short of complete success?

Dorothy Rowe places some of the responsibility for this price on the psychologists themselves, observing that:

> Psychiatrists and psychologists are, on the whole, an irreligious lot, and as such are untypical of the general population. Surveys show that between 60 and 90 per cent of the population in the UK and the USA believe in God and in a relationship between God and human goodness and wickedness.
>
> Thus most of the people who come to psychiatrists and psychologists for help are not asking 'How can I be happy?' — but 'How can I be good?'

PART II

BEYOND PSYCHOLOGY

A physicist is an atom's way of knowing about atoms.

G. Wald

=== 4 ===

THE NEW SCIENCE

Here we are — so what must the universe be?

John Wheeler

If, as seems strongly indicated, current psychology goes just so far and no further to provide definitive answers to human needs and aspirations, where is the next logical direction to extend the search, to look for more effective and practicable solutions to the here-and-now of daily life?

The most obvious, most logical and immediate direction must lie beyond circumscribed human conditioning with its conformity to prevailing 'norms', and in those larger vistas of life, those evident or non-evident laws of universal action, which underpin and run the cosmos itself, with or without man.

These laws, however, have a double aspect: man is both dependent on what scientific laws can contribute to technological progress, and its attendant comforts, and reluctant to connect with the question of their initial source. While deferring to the wonders of science, man seems to remain blinkered to its possible relevance for him, clinging with perhaps unconscious tenacity to concern for 'the economy', 'society', local or global politics, the pursuit of 'human rights'.

As Carl Sagan points out:

> We go about our daily lives understanding almost nothing of the world. We give little thought to the machinery that generates the sunlight that makes life possible, to the gravity that glues us to an Earth that would otherwise send us spinning off into space, or to the atoms of which we are made and on whose stability we fundamentally depend.

41

This double aspect of dependence and reluctance might not need probing for significance if psychology alone had been able to shed more light on what was involved in the phenomenon of human life itself, its relationship to that which created it out of itself.

Silently, by the millions and perhaps billions, individual man has some sense of connection to underlying laws and may give it the name of 'God', but expressed or unexpressed, the only avenue of exploration for further proof or enlightenment rests inexorably in consideration of these laws and what they are.

Laws are apparent in every element of life as a regulating order in process: the sequence of seasons, the oceanic tides, cycles of weather, the principle of electricity (which can execute a man or cook his dinner), magnetic attraction, the interplay of mass and energy (matter and workforce), gravity and equilibrium, balance (try riding a bicycle without it!), and many more. Is it too conjectural to posit some all-embracing, unified law that differs only in the infinite variety or multiplicity of its forms or expression, thereby justifying it as a source of practical enquiry?

In today's science, which has superseded without entirely excluding earlier concepts of classical or 'mechanistic' science (which sees the universe as purely objective and physical with no need in it for man or 'God'), there is a revolutionary new approach to this question, a new focus on the role of man in the universe, and a searchlight of exploration for a 'Unified Field Theory' (one which Albert Einstein sought to the end of his life without success) such as has heretofore been the singular province of 'metaphysics'. Known as Quantum Theory, it deals with atomic physics (the science of the infinitely small), and is partly described in this way by Fritjof Capra:

> The subatomic units of matter are very abstract entities which have a dual aspect. Depending on how we look at them, they appear sometimes as particles, sometimes as waves; and this dual nature is also exhibited by light which can take the form of electromagnetic waves or particles — i.e. an entity confined to a very small volume — and a wave, which is spread out over a large region of space. This contradiction gave rise to most of the koan-like paradoxes which finally led to the formulation of quantum theory.
>
> The whole development started when Max Planck discovered that the energy heat radiation is not emitted continuously, but appears in the form of 'energy packets'.

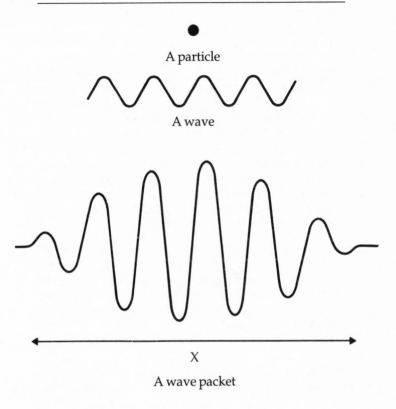

A particle

A wave

A wave packet

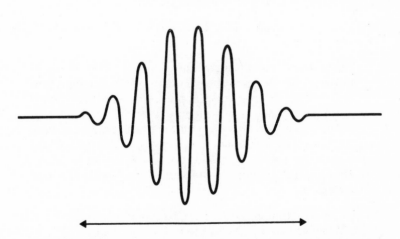

Squeezing the wave packet into a smaller region

Einstein called these energy packets 'quanta' and recognised them as a fundamental aspect of nature.

Later discoveries showed that at the subatomic level, matter does not exist with certainty at definite places, but rather 'shows tendencies to occur'. In quantum theory these tendencies are expressed as 'probabilities', and are associated with mathematical quantities which take the form of waves.

This, says Fritjof Capra, is why particles can be waves at the same time. They are not 'real' three-dimensional waves like sound or water waves. They are 'probability' waves, abstract mathematical quantities with all the characteristic properties of waves which are related to the probabilities of finding the particles at particular points in space and at particular times.

> We can never predict an atomic event with certainty: we can only say how likely it is to happen...and ultimately these patterns do not represent probabilities of things, but rather probabilities of interconnections...interconnections between the preparation of an experiment and the subsequent measurement...
>
> Quantum theory reveals a basic oneness of the universe. It shows that we cannot decompose the world into independently existing smallest units. As we penetrate into matter, nature does not show us any 'isolated basic building blocks', but rather appears as a complicated web of relations between the various parts of the whole.

The crucial revelation implicit here, has been the distinct new role of man, for as Fritjof Capra goes on to say:

> These revelations always include the observer in an essential way. The human observer constitutes the final link in the chain of observational processes, and the properties of any atomic object can only be understood in terms of the object's interaction with the observer. This means that the classical ideal of an objective description of nature is no longer valid...In atomic physics, we can never speak about nature without at the same time, speaking about ourselves.

Going even further in the essential flaw of objective detachment, John Wheeler has suggested the following:

> Nothing is more important about the quantum principle than this, that it destroys the concept of the world as 'sit-

ting out there', with the observer safely separated from it by a 20 centimer slab of plate glass. Even to observe so minuscule an object as an electron, he must shatter the glass. He must reach in. He must install his chosen measuring equipment. It is up to him to decide whether he shall measure position or momentum. To install the equipment to measure the one prevents and excludes his installing the equipment to measure the other. Moreover, the measurement changes the state of the electron. The universe will never afterwards be the same. To describe what has happened, one has to cross out that old word 'observer' and put in its place the new word 'participator'. In some strange sense the universe is a participatory universe.

Leading ever onwards, David Bohm attributes the delay and impediment in general understanding of this 'seamless garment' of life's basic unity to its persistent 'fragmentation' by the long-held mechanistic view, which studied every facet of existence in isolation, separate and apart from any other, giving the intensity and specialization of its exploration absolute priority.

Once this fragmentation is examined and seen as a limiting factor, the whole canvas of life can be looked at in a new light.

Calling his own theory, 'the implicate order', David Bohm carries the idea of a universal inseparability, one in which man could not possibly be outside because there is no outside, to a 'wholeness' in which all action, potential and creative expression is 'enfolded', and therefore must always be working its way through all that is.

Many scientists have spent their entire lives examining and analysing what is known as the 'big bang' theory. This presupposes a time when the universe exploded into existence, before which it did not exist. The process by which it reached this stage still pervades the frontier of theoretical physics, as does what Stephen Hawking has so relentlessly explored: the 'what-exactly-happened with the "early universe" of the moment before the big bang.'

In his most recent conclusions, Stephen Hawking has, in his own words, 'changed his mind':

Einstein's general theory of relativity implied that the universe must have a beginning and, possibly, an end! (This was to be the starting point for my work in theoretical physics...

Nowadays nearly everyone assumes that the universe started with a big bang singularity...It is perhaps ironic that, having changed my mind, I am not trying to convince other physicists that there was no singularity at the beginning of the universe...it can disappear once quantum effects are taken into account...

In less than half a century, man's view of the universe, formed over a millennia, has been transformed. When the theory of general relativity broke down, we were forced to turn our search for an understanding of the universe from the extraordinarily vast to the extraordinarily tiny.

Having departed from his initial anti-God, anti-mystical stance (mysticism, he commented, was a 'cop-out' for not having sufficient comprehension of the four fundamental forces of classical physics — gravity, the electro-magnetic force, and the so-called 'weak' and 'strong' nuclear forces), he came to consider that gravity:

> shapes the large-scale structure of the universe, even though it is the weakest of the four categories. The new possibility was that space and time together might form a finite, four-dimensional space without singularities or boundaries like the surface of the earth, but with more dimensions...This could explain many of the observed features of the universe, such as its large-scale uniformity and also the smaller-scale departures from homogeneity, like galaxies, stars, and even human beings. But if the universe is completely self-contained, with no singularities or boundaries, and completely described by a unified theory, that has profound implications for the role of God as Creator.

Finally, Stephen Hawking says: 'We still believe that the universe should be logical and beautiful; we just dropped the word "God".' Has he dropped it back when he now says:

> If we do discover a complete theory, it should in time be understandable in broad principle by everyone, not just a few scientists. Then we would all, philosophers, scientists, and just ordinary people, be able to take part in the discussion of the question of why it is that we and the universe exist. If we find the answer to that, it would be the ultimate triumph of human reason — for then we would know the mind of God.

There are other theories, some conflicting, some still 'on the fence' and some radically original, such as Rupert Sheldrake's hypothesis of 'formative causation' that everything in the universe resonates with itself without reference to direct information or distance in a timeless omnipresence. However, this is doubtless a time of moving on, beyond what has gone before, toward the possibilities of new answers to old questions.

5

THE LAW OF GROWTH

> What is it that both perceives the material world
> and at the same time subjectively knows its own
> existence?
>
> Sir Alister Hardy

Now that the New Science has discovered that man, in his physical exploration of the nature of the universe, affects it by the very act of his observation, what is his next direction in the search for resolution of his daily experience? How, he may now want to ask, has this stage of self-awareness come about? How has he travelled from an unconscious evolutionary process to consciousness of himself as participant in his own development?

It is easy enough to retrace the manifest sequence of the Law of Growth that brought him from an organism to a species called *Homo sapiens*. First, there were uncountable billions of every variety of life-form, the varieties themselves without limit of sbape, size, or colouring. Millennia of the global-scale extinction of individual life made it appear totally expendable, its only survivors being, in evolutionary terms, 'of the fittest'.

However, if this is so, self-observing man speculates, *why*? Was there more than ruthless biological indifference at work, more than the generation of unlimited numbers as the fundamental substance of a physical universe?

'So careful of the type, she seems,' said Alfred Lord Tennyson, 'so careless of the single life.'

Could it be that there was another law in process, a law of averages — a law that preserves its type, or species, by creating it in such vast quantities as to ensure the survival of the 'single life'? And once the single life is established, does it emerge from the law of averages enabled to act on its own behalf, free of the physical rule of the law of growth?

In retrospect, man can now speculate about this emergence, can observe that he is conscious of being self-conscious. He sees that although many other species survived and became specialized, they did not become conscious of themselves. A dog may share some instincts and feeling with man, and is capable of learning and responding, but is not conscious of being a dog. It may recognize other dogs, and sense the difference between itself and a cat, but is not capable of considering its own existence.

Man, then, at least on this planet, seems to be unique in having arrived at a stage of self-conscious evolution, which suggests an unfolding of an underlying, invisible plan or principle rather than one that is solely physically generated. The implications of this are many: man sees that he can determine the direction of his own life, that responsibility for his own experience no longer depends on chance but can be decided by his own actions and choices.

It is like starting all over again, so new to his former concept of himself in relation to the world in which he lives that he must first crawl, then walk, before he can run in a direction he wants to go. He becomes more acutely cognizant of the way in which he is influenced by the beliefs and opinions of others, by what he has himself believed, and begins to recognize the contradictions in his estimate of what is real or not real, true or not true, worthwhile or irrelevant.

It may occur to him to look into the continuing effect of what still lies beneath his conscious awareness, to the instinctual roots of his development that must still be present and at work in his reactions and behaviour. Why does he have all kinds of ailments of the body as well as emotional confusion? What is the link between 'cosmic stuff' and 'mind stuff', between the brain as a computer, translator or organizer of a chemically based life, and mind as the origin of the brain for purposes of translation and selection of its wholeness.

Is it any wonder that the mind-body question is so subtle as to be practically indecipherable?

In his book *Quantum Healing*, Deepak Chopra speaks of the advent of 'neuro-transmitters', which are a 'new class of minute chemicals which transmit nerve impulses and act in our bodies as "communicator molecules" whereby the neurons of the brain can talk to the rest of the body.'

They are the runners that race to and from the brain, telling every organ inside us of our emotions, desires, memories, intuitions and dreams. None of these are confined to the brain alone...

Likewise none of them are strictly mental, since they can be coded into chemical messages. Neuro-transmitters touch the life of every cell. Wherever a thought wants to go, these chemicals must go, too, and without them, no thought can exist. To think is to practice brain chemistry, promoting a cascade of responses throughout the body. We see that intelligence, as know-how, pervades the physiology — now it has acquired a material basis.

He concludes that:

If every cell has an endless number of messages it can send and receive, it is also clear that only a small fraction are activated at one time. Who or what controls the messages? That turns out to be an explosive question. In a chemistry lab, reactions will run automatically as soon as the experiment starts; it is just a matter of mixing one chemical with another. Yet, someone has to take the chemicals off the shelf... Now we see that with thousands of chemicals on its shelf, a cell has not only to choose some, mix them together, and analyse the results. It has to make the chemicals in the first place, finding thousands of ways to create new molecules out of basically a handful of elements — carbon, hydrogen, oxygen and nitrogen. To do that requires a mind. For the first time in the history of science, mind has a visible scaffold to stand upon. Before this, science declared that we are physical machines that have somehow learned to think. Now it dawns that we are thoughts that have learned to create a physical machine.

Carrying this interpretation into everyday terms as man attempts to cope with his dismaying variety of physical ailments, is it of much practical use to know that they may not be of physical origin? Do the symptoms dissolve with the intellectual acceptance that mind might have created the problem?

In the realm of 'psychosomatic' medicine, for instance, there has been increasing evidence of a causal connection between what is felt and thought and what is experienced as a physical symptom. Can it contribute light on this question?

Doctor A.T.W. Simeons, among others in this field, has described how the 'old brain-stem' inherited from the time when the evolution of life forms developed the first sensory means of survival, still exists in the brain of modern man. In fact, without this old brain-stem, the two hemispheres of the modern brain would be completely useless:

> As the brain-stem runs all the basic manifestations of life, it would be impossible to remove it and leave the hemisphere intact as this would result in instantaneous death.

But it is the 'diencephalon' that is the most important part of the brain-stem. This is where all the regulatory adjustments of the body have their origin. Lying roughly in the middle of the brain, in the diencephalon animal instincts such as fear, rage, hunger, and sex are translated into physiological activity. Here, originally, the basic senses of hearing and seeing developed to decide what action should be taken in response to the approach of danger, or possible attack. The main responses were flight, concealment, or defence. For these there came the needed rise in blood sugar, an increase in pulse rate, salivation, and a flood of gastric juice in the stomach.

These responses or reactions have given man the designation of 'the timid animal'. Timidity was the preliminary of evasion and withdrawal from the size, strength, and physical superiority of other species. Later, as messages of warning did not always require immediate action, only the readiness for it, the memory of the warnings was stored, and a form of censorship gradually established which 'screened' the sense information, leaving a choice of response. This led to the necessity of a new structure to the existing brain with far more capacity for handling the increase of deliberation involved — namely the cortex or 'grey matter'.

The growth of the 'thinking' cortex was phenomenally rapid. While the earlier phases of evolution took tens of millions of years, the later phases were covered in a few hundred thousand years. At first this accelerated evolutionary leap did not disrupt the harmonious coordination of the old and the new. The cortex and brain-stem were, as Doctor Simeons put it, 'a highly satisfactory means of assuring survival and evolutionary prosperity, as it still is in all *wild-living* mammals.'

However, he adds:

> When about half a million years ago, man began very slowly to embark upon the road to cultural advance, an entirely new situation arose. The use of implements and the control of fire introduced artefacts of which the cortex

could avail itself for the purpose of living. These artefacts had no relationship whatever to the organization of the body and could, therefore, not be integrated into the functioning of the brain-stem...

The diencephalon continued to function just as if the artefacts were non-existent...The instinctive behaviour ceased to be appropriate...thus the diencephalon goes into its normal emergency routine. It raises the pulse rate, the blood pressure and the blood sugar; it stops hunger and may produce a liquid evacuation of the bowel; it may raise gooseflesh and will tense the muscles. All the old reactions to fear have rendered the natural instinctive reaction unnecessary.

In modern civilization it is almost never admitted or even known that the emotion of fear still calls out the diencephalon with the same effects on the body. The cortex does not say, 'Thank you, but go away, I can handle this.' Suppressed, unidentified, the preparations for flight, fight or hiding continue to operate as numberless physical symptoms — high blood pressure, bronchial asthma, bowel problems, palpitations, leg cramps, paralysis of limbs — as well as the depression of unexpressed anger. In sum, as Doctor Simeons describes it, there is almost no form of emotion-based human feeling that does not have its physical counterpart.

All in all, can awareness of these aspects of man's evolution help improve the quality of existence?

It is not easy to live in a society where not only is it against the law to hit another person when aroused for defence, but socially unwise; nor is it easy to stand and confront an enemy when the aroused instinct is for flight. As for hiding in the face of danger, in an office situation where there is a threat of redundancy, the effect would be ridiculous. Yet the frustration of these instinctive functions accounts for much of civilized man's emotional stress, nameless pervading anxieties and related illnesses.

Since the physical evolutionary principle is demonstrably never regressive, the effects of the diencephalon must eventually be overcome by the ever-developing cortex. Many may suffer *en route*, but can now both take into account and proceed with aware consideration of what created the brain in the first place.

As a result, one will be impelled to consider the genesis of life itself. Is it possible, one might now ask, that the physical laws that appear to be the source as well as the process of evolving life in all its forms, are in fact based in some invisible, initiating 'blueprint' that reflects into physical manifestation?

Perhaps once again what is needed is another evolutionary 'leap' to encompass greater insights and comprehension. As John C. Lilly has said:

> The miracle is that the universe created a part of itself to study the rest of it.

Nothing is more obvious and unquestionable than that *consciousness*, for man in his personal frame of reference, is the one and only place for him to keep looking for enlightenment. Where else? With what else can he investigate himself?

His main goal, his main objective, must be to bring everything within himself into consciousness, up from the enveloping fog and impenetrable shadow into the sharp light of scrutiny. Painful, frightening, bafflingly complex, engendering more imponderable questions than it can answer, consciousness is yet the indispensable and vital instrument of man's advancement. As Jacob Needleman describes it so well:

> A conscious universe is the only reality which can include human consciousness. Only a conscious universe is relevant to the whole of human life.

= 6 =

RELATING THE PART TO THE WHOLE, THE WHOLE TO THE PART

Experiences which seem remote from each other in the individual are perhaps all equally near in the universal.

Edward Carpenter

Exciting and significant as is the promise of the New Science to relate the whole to the part, the part to the whole, it is probably more fraught with pitfalls than any other form of research. For if science does the meta-physical stretching of its former limits, it may lose its credibility, thus losing a majority of its own members. Even the most careful elaboration and illustration of a mental physical marriage of opposites, has implicit dangers.

Ken Wilber warns against these, which he calls 'pop mysticism':

> I find honest work almost overwhelmed by the buzz of absolutely crazy ideas being put forth with the aim of establishing a link between quantum mechanics and mysticism...already many physicists are furious with the 'mystical' use to which particle physics is being subjected ...
>
> Let them [physics and mysticism] appreciate each other and let their dialogue and mutual exchange of ideas never cease. But unwarranted and premature marriages usually end in divorce. And all too often a divorce that terribly damages both parties.

Ravi Ravindra also points out a crucial hazard in any stand for the inseparability between ancient philosophical and spiritual systems and quantum physics of the West:

Perception is very important in both physics and (for instance) yoga: they are both looking for objective knowledge, and they are both interested in empirical verification. They are experimental or experiential and empirical. I think this is true. But let me...draw a distinction; in order to have clarity, it is important not to slide over these distinctions between two words, *experiment* and *experience*. I wish to stress that the modern natural sciences are thoroughly experimental in character, but they are in fact almost determinedly contra-experiential...

In physics, experimental data, observations and perceptions are all in the service of theory. What we ultimately end up calling scientific knowledge is an ensemble of theories. Whereas, completely by contrast, the point of theory in any spiritual disciple is that it is in the service of perception. And it ultimately doesn't matter very much what theory one has. Theory is a device, a trick to quieten the mind or engage the mind, or enlarge the mind...

To imagine that our science of today is equivalent to ancient esoteric knowledge, presumably because of some superficial similarities in some expressions, is an indication of complete ignorance of the methods and aims of ancient spiritual traditions. Implicit in these sentimental assertions of similarity and equivalence is a naive and arrogant assumption that tomorrow — next decade, next century, or surely the next millennium — our science will far surpass the ancient mystics, sages and prophets.

Fritjof Capra's whole book, *The Tao of Physics*, is committed to examples of the similarities and parallels between Western science and Eastern mysticism. However, he does not hold that there can be a synthesis in which physicists abandon the scientific method and begin to meditate. Rather, he sees science and mysticism as 'two complementary manifestations of the human mind: of its rational and intuitive faculties. The modern physicist experiences the world through extreme specialization of the rational mind; the mystic through extreme specialization of the intuitive mind... Neither is comprehended in the other, nor can either of them be reduced to the other, but both are necessary, supplementing one another for a full understanding of the world... Science does not need mysticism and mysticism does not need science; but man needs both.'

He goes on to say that as of today the 'dynamic interplay' needed between mystical intuition and scientific analysis has not been achieved in our society, and most physicists still actively support a mechanistic, fragmented world-view 'without seeing that science points beyond such a view, towards a oneness of the universe which includes not only our natural environment but also our fellow human beings. To radically change this a whole cultural revolution, in the true sense of the word, must take place. The survival of our whole civilization may depend on whether we can bring about such a change.'

What is being asked in this context is not so much whether the study of nuclear physics or the ancient systems of 'interior science', either separately or together, are right or essential to the resolution of man's here-and-now troubles and needs, but whether within mystic experience the experience of 'bliss' is guaranteed to heal all psychological wounds.

The answer to this can never be entirely clear — except to those who have experienced it — for mystic experience is wholly and purely experiential. It can be described, and has been throughout human history — and the language of its description, which is always the same despite the background or education of the experiencer, is its only 'body of evidence'. No one can take the experience away from the one who has had it: that person *knows*. The experimenter, the researcher, the scientist may write about it, elaborate on it, but unless at some time he has found himself experiencing it as well, he will only be speaking *about* it. The radiance described, the love, the 'rightness' of the universe, the peace, the benevolence, the joy, the 'bliss' beyond all words will be locked into the private consciousness of the experiencer.

How can this help the ordinary person with ordinary problems who may be finding it difficult to get through the night, may be trapped in addiction, suicidally depressed, out of control of his aggression or fears?

It is one thing to understand, intellectually, that a life-force, a 'presence' that can be called 'God', has been known to lift the invalid from his bed, return the terminally ill to health, has enabled ordinary people to perform miraculous feats of strength, but it is another to so believe in this power that it can be called into immediate use. Intellectually, then, man does not have much difficulty in considering his own mystery; it is only when he is more convinced of his separateness, his insignificance, his expendability, that he comes to an impasse.

How can he relate the part to the whole? How can the whole be seen by him to relate to the part? Can it perhaps be thought of, felt as, a 'mirroring effect'? Joseph Chilton Pearce suggests that:

There is a relationship between what we *think* is out there in the world and what we experience as being out there. There is a way in which the energy of thought and the energy of matter modify each other and interrelate. A kind of rough mirroring takes place between our mind and our reality.

We cannot stand outside this mirroring process and examine it, though, for we *are* the process, to an unknowable extent. Any technique we might use to 'look objectively' at our reality becomes a part of the event in question. We are an indeterminately large part of the function that shapes the reality from which we do our looking. Our looking enters as one of the determinants in the reality event that we see...

William Blake claimed that perception was the universal, the perceived object was the particular. What is discovered by man is never the 'universal' or 'cosmic truth'. Rather, the *process* by which the mind brings about a 'discovery' is itself the universal. Thus a change of world view can change the world view.

While this may be appreciated as supportive evidence of the interrelatedness of man with that which made him (in which the eye sees itself seeing, as well as being that which is seen), is it a principle he can rely on to supply him with concrete guidance for making human decisions, acquitting himself in human crises, for raising the level of his human desires and aspirations? How does he equate his universality with his transcience? How does he go about being an abstract, undifferentiated, unindividualized form of an omnipresent, omniscient, omnipotent, self-creating, self-knowing, self-contemplating, creative cosmic principle and substance, which both surrounds him and works through him?

The answer must lie somewhere within man's capacity for self-exploration. Blind acceptance of ideologies and faiths may have to be brought into awareness and re-examined. Man may need to begin a self-inquisition to find out just where he stands in his own eyes, where his prejudices lurk undetected, just what fears design his actions and attitudes, direct his life-experience.

What, in the final analysis, does he truly and actually believe about himself, about mankind, about the universe?

Once this 'spring-cleaning' of his consciousness has been tackled, he may be half-way to making room for some new clarity, and, whether he finds himself aligned with the 'God' principle of religion, or the mathematically 'elegant' principle of science, or the metaphysical Alpha-Omega of both, he will be able to chart his course with greater precision to discern the absolute in the relative, the impersonal in the personal.

Not until man has become aware of himself as inseparable from that which has created him out of itself, by means of its own laws, will he know without doubt whether he is mortal or immortal, whether he is to be lost forever with his bones and ashes, or to live on *ad infinitum* in ever-expanding dimensions of being.

7

THE PERSONAL FACTOR

The relationship of the one to the many, the part to
the whole, is a matter of current concern to both
science and metaphysics, so that one can deeply
appreciate not only the influence of the collective
state of consciousness upon the individual, but also
the effect of an individual's transformation upon
the collective state of consciousness.

W. Brugh Joy

For the majority of people who give thought to the largest questions of their existence — What is life? Who am I in relation to
it? Is there, or is there not a power greater than man that rules
the universe in all its manifestations? — the view most common
to all is that whatever differences of belief may be held, the fundamental nature of life is *impersonal*. The laws of science are physically impersonal; the laws of 'God' are divinely impersonal.

The possibility of the impersonal becoming personal takes up
a vast amount of space in sacred literature and forms the prepon-
derant substance of prayer in Western religions. In Eastern philosophies, where there is no personal supplication to the cosmos,
it is detachment from desire that resolves the whole-and-part interaction.

To the average person in search of help in coping and manag-
ing, stumbling along in a twilight of contradictory interpretations,
thoughts and feelings, the impersonal may be too remote to offer
immediate sustenance. On the other hand, if there *was* some way
for the impersonal to become personal, intimate, it might prove
to be just what is needed — the missing piece in the puzzle, the
life-raft in the ocean of doubt.

But how is this 'personal factor' to be ascertained, let alone put to use? Approaches to this question abound, some age-old, some newly presented: meditation, silent contemplation, words of ancient wisdom, the tenets of religious faiths, writings of philosophers, and so on.

Any one, or any combination of all of these avenues of exploration are potential areas of discovery of what is sometimes called the law of reciprocity: here the impersonal universe responds to the personal by becoming it; or, put another way, by individualizing its unindividualized wholeness. The very concept of 'person' is to be seen as implicit in the whole, and not, as is commonly felt, one that sets man apart, without anchor in a cosmic impersonality. Rather, the individual 'person' is a logical extension or translation of an indivisible whole, an archetypal person, working as a two-way law.

If this can be comprehended, man may begin to overcome an ingrained belief that the great impersonal universe could not possible have any interest in his personal fate. He can feel himself involved in a unity that presupposes support and caring.

The next inquiry is: how to put the personal factor to use. This requires far more than an intellectual grasp. It demands a conscious, knowing, trial-and-error experimentation. If it is to make the vital difference so urgently needed for any real and durable grip on individual experience, it must prove itself in action. The pious intent, the rituals, the sermonizing and preaching of a thousand salesmen of a 'new age', all telling the rest of humanity how best to serve it, fills the airwaves, the literature, the pulpits of contemporary life.

However, man may first need to ask: what exactly is the 'personal'? Perhaps it can be safely said that emotion is personal, feeling is personal, opinion is personal. In impersonal terms these would be expressed as thought energy moving through an individual thinker, becoming 'personalness'. 'Love', as an impersonal fundament of creation, becomes personal, by means of its law or response, which is never arbitrary, always a non-dual interaction.

One may now ask what is the function of this 'personal factor' as it appears to human beings. In the words of Thomas Troward:

> The function of the Personal Factor in the Creative Order is to provide specialized conditions by the use of the powers of *Selection* and *Initiative*, a truth indicated by the maxim 'Nature unaided fails'. . .the function of the Personal Factor is to analyze the manifestations of Law which are spontaneously afforded by nature and to discover the Universal Affirmative Principle which lies hidden within

them, and then by the exercise of our powers of Initiative and Selection to provide such specialized conditions as will enable the Universal Principle to work in perfectly new ways transcending anything in our past experience.

Here, however, Thomas Troward adds:

> This is how all progress has been achieved up to the present; and is the way in which all progress must be achieved in the future, only for the purpose of evolution, or growth from within, we must transfer the method to the spiritual plane.

What is proposed is not unfamiliar but unequivocal: in order for man to put the personal factor to the test, to verify and confirm its effect and ensure its value to his daily experience, fundamental acceptance of a 'spiritual plane' is demanded.

Is this an impasse beyond which man can no longer travel without commitment? It is said that 'to be conscious at all, one must be conscious of something'. What is man to be conscious of? If he does not investigate, he will never be sure of the answer. As Thomas Troward concludes: 'It is like trying to climb up a ladder that is resting against nothing.'

PART III

CONSCIOUS THINKING

The universe as a whole could have a cause and a purpose only if it were itself created by a conscious agent which transcended it. Unlike the universe, this transcendent consciousness would not be developing towards a goal; it would be its own goal. It would not be striving towards a final form; it would be complete within itself.

Rupert Sheldrake

8

THE PRINCIPLE IN PRACTICE

What we know is not much: what we do not know is immense.

Pierre Laplace

From all the foregoing surveys and observations, despite their omissions and sketchiness, it has become obvious that man's search for just where he fits into the 'grand scheme' of life requires some form of concrete evidence. It is said that mankind comes into this world with too little information, but it is surely counter-productive to claim to know the truth of what is missing. Where, man continues to ask, can tangible proof be found? — Not just the 'signs and wonders' looked for since the beginning of his search for certainty, but some immediate and irrefutable confirmation of faith made manifest. Since all principles are invisibly founded, what is sought can only be proved in practice. Until faith is tried, it cannot be proven.

How and in what way, then, can man find the faith in himself to provide the proof? Or is it the other way round: should he, in one abandoned plunge, dive into the deep-end, the high-risk area of his inner life? After all, there is nothing whatsoever to be lost. He needs to know nothing but the principle, to practise it, and to watch the results in his experience.

Although the intellect may lead him to it with ease, the *principle* must be well understood. This could take time and perseverance, will (not willpower) and determination. Not a great price to pay for the beginning of control of one's own life.

Please note that from this point on, the presentation of the subject also becomes 'personal'.

MAKING ABSTRACT TRUTH PRACTICAL

In essence, this is the principle of the personal factor. We want to put the intelligence behind all creation into practice in our daily lives, to make use of it rather than to just acknowledge its possibilities. Ernest Holmes has said, 'We would better spend our time using the Law than arguing over it.'

We have seen that all the theories and arguments in history have never been able to pinpoint the exact way in which mind is conscious, subconscious or unconscious. Perhaps our thought vibrates into form, or perhaps it is electromagnetic, drawing all that is like itself towards itself; we really cannot know.

The only thing that we can know is that when we apply the principle with deliberate intent, it produces results that can be seen in our personal lives. We can test and experiment with it by alternately applying it or not applying it, by thinking in the random way in which most of us are accustomed, or by thinking consciously — in other words, in a way that will demonstrate what we want to experience, rather than that which we do not.

The law of the subconscious mind can be compared with the soil which, when we place a seed in it, cannot argue as to whether or not it is a good seed, or whether it wants to grow that particular seed, but must at once go to work to produce it as a plant. It has no choice, cannot say it would rather grow a potato than a carrot, yet provides all the appropriate chemicals and conditions necessary for the growth of the seed. No one knows, except by long experience with seeds, just what kind of plant each little wizened looking object will turn out to be. There is no clue in the seed of the rose to the beauty and fragrance of its blossom. The idea of the rose is implicit in the seed. No living person could have conceived the idea. That which is the conceiver of all that exists contains the blueprint.

In this way the subconscious level of mind receives the seed-idea implanted by the conscious mind (or 'spirit'), and must go to work to produce it in kind, as effect, condition, results, experience. It responds to the 'Word' — by corresponding to it, precisely, 'literally'. It has no sense of humour, cannot be fooled, is mechanically set into motion. It is the infinite intelligence in action.

On the other hand, the law of mind is not without intelligence. While it does not reason or discriminate, it has the entire creative medium of the universe with which to build. There is no distance or time to hinder it: it always knows how, even if it can never say why. Over the centuries it has been called 'the servant of the spirit', a 'blind force, knowing only to do, never to question'. The sub-conscious law is the executor of the command of the conscious mind, the means by which the conscious becomes the thing it has conceived.

The process is this: infinite mind, by nature creative, is forever creating ideas of itself, out of itself, by means of its own law. It does this in order to experience itself, to re-'cognize' itself in the particular, the part, the degree. To this end, it must take form. Only through form can it express its formless whole. Only in individualizing its unindividualized totality can it enjoy its own nature. This, approximately, is what is meant by 'we are made in the image and likeness of God'.

This brings us again to the semantics of the term 'God'.

THE ROLE OF 'GOD' IN CONSCIOUS THINKING

A great obstacle can be removed from full understanding, as well as resistance to the word 'God' by re-assessing what is really meant by it. Intrinsically, it matters not whether it has a religious associ-ation, *here* it has only one service — to symbolize or be a syno-nym for any or all of the following: the First Cause; the Uncreated; the Absolute or Unconditioned; the One and Only Life; Creative Energy; the One Mind; Infinite Intelligence; Essence of Being; Life-Force; Spirit; Supreme Principle; Originating Mind; Omnipotent Mind, Self-Knowing Mind; Creator of All that Is; the One and Only Power; Beingness; Atman Brahman; 'Isness'; and many, many others of limitless variation.

The main objective is to cleanse our consciousness of all but the basic concept of a creative intelligence fundamental to life. God is not a form of any kind whatever, cannot be found in any one shape. God is only evidenced; everything is God, manifest or unmanifest. So when we say, I am God in this form of itself, it means only that there is nothing else I can be, or anyone can be, or any thing. The use of the word becomes as descriptive as that of those more neutral sounding terms given above. Without being blasphemous we can say, there is not God and me — there is God *as* me. Thus does the last trace of an anthropomorphic God dis-solve, and the impersonal God of cosmic laws become personal to each and every one of us.

For this reason, we no longer pray to a God outside ourselves. We no longer supplicate, bargain, atttempt to win merit, placate with rites and rituals — we turn within ourselves and listen to the 'still small voice' that speaks from our own inseparable source by means of 'insights' and '*in*-tuition'. This voice is personal to us, but speaks from infinite wisdom, ultimate knowledge, and, the unconditioned love of its own creation, which must include 'you'.

We have now brought the power of an omnipotent creator into our individualizing consciousness, tapped into its availability through our awareness of its being there. We have done what it is necessary to do to gain its specific response — and we have begun to listen.

And now, as we turn up the volume, we find that the same absolute law which has created and runs the universe may be ours to use in the ordering of our personal lives. It authorizes the macrocosm, we authorize the microcosm. It is the big circle without circumference, ours the small circle within it which moves forward towards its unreachable horizon.

We are, therefore, co-creators with God, or that which made us.

THE CREATIVE PROCESS

The creative process works as a 'trinity', clarified by a close study of these Charts (Figures 4-7). Everything that is manifest starts in the invisible realm of mind, or spirit. First, the infinite contemplates itself, conceives an idea of itself, and this idea or conception becomes law to its manifestation. As these metaphysical charts show, there are: Creative Intelligence; Creative Medium; Result (Effect, Body, Form, Experience). Just as infinite, self-knowing intelligence 'gives birth' to forms of itself, so do we give birth by the same law to the forms of our ideas. We see what we believe 'outpictured' in the circumstances of our current lives. We have believed that they just 'happened' to us, are part of the way life is, an uphill struggle, a battle of good and evil, unavoidable catastrophes, chance, accident, injustice, the inquities of the current government, society, the time we live in — or by 'acts of God' without mercy, and by all the inherent cruelties that lie just below the surface of our civilized veneer. We see ourselves as victims of fate, with no possibility of influencing outer events — 'When my number is on it', we say, 'that will be it'.

Most of us have been conditioned from infancy to believe that happiness is fleeting and carries a price. We do not feel a right to claim it, and if it becomes a possibility, we look behind in anticipation of an axe that must surely fall.

The connection between what happens to us 'out there' and what we have been thinking and believing 'in here' is seldom

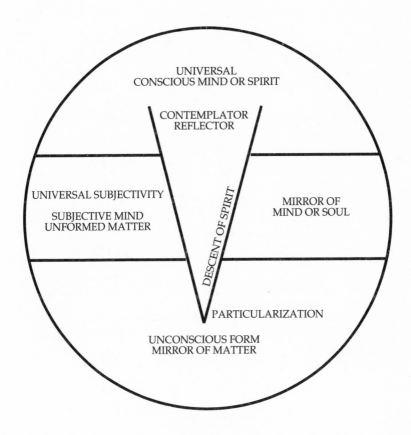

Figure 4 Metaphysical Chart 1: The upper section of this chart shows how the conscious mind, or spirit of man, reflects or contemplates itself, through the medium of soul or subjectivity, into form or matter. The middle section represents the World-Soul or Subjectivity; the Mirror of Mind and unformed matter; the Servant of the Spirit; the lower section shows the result of self-contemplation as it takes form in the world of matter.

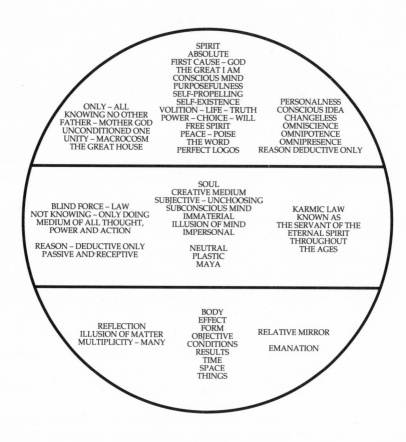

Figure 5 Metaphysical Chart 2: This chart, which is called the Universal Chart, shows the Universe as a Trinity of Being. The upper section designates those attributes of Spirit which are Self-Conscious. The middle section shows the subconscious aspect of Law; and the lower section shows the effect of Spirit working through the medium of Universal Mind.

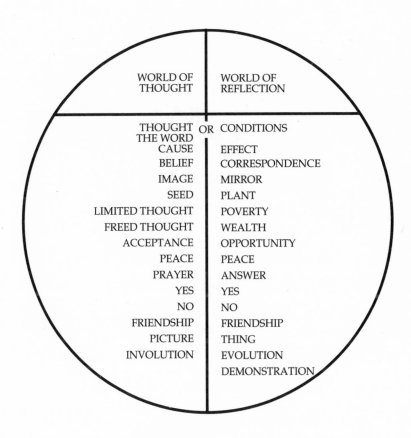

Figure 6 Metaphysical Chart 3: How ideas manifest as things. This chart is divided into two sides, representing the world of thought and the world of reflections. It represents the law of cause and effect. The world of thought is the world of ideas, while the world of reflections means the results of thought. The world of reflections is entirely a world of effects and is, of itself, unconscious and unknowing. Consider everything on the left side of this chart to be thoughts or ideas; and consider everything on the right side to be the automatic results of the law as it works out into effects.

71

THE TRIUNE UNITY
THE INDIVISIBLE WHOLE –
WITHIN WHICH IS ALL OF ITS PARTS
THE ABSOLUTE WITHIN WHICH IS THE RELATIVE
THE UNCREATED WITHIN WHICH IS THE CREATED
THE CHANGELESS WITHIN WHICH IS ALL CHANGE
THE FORMLESS WITHIN WHICH IS ALL FORM
THE LIMITLESS WITHIN WHICH IS ALL SPACE
THE TIMELESS WITHIN WHICH IS ALL TIME
THE UNIVERSAL WITHIN WHICH IS THE INDIVIDUAL
THE ONE PERSON WITHIN WHOM ARE ALL PEOPLE
SOURCE AND CENTRE OF ALL LIFE POWER AND ACTION
TRUTH, LOVE, MIND, SPIRIT, THE EVER, AND THE ALL

PERSONALITY ... INDIVIDUALITY

MAN

Figure 7 Metaphysical Chart 4: In this chart it is shown that the Absolute contains the relative, within Itself, but is not limited by the relative. The relative does not limit, but expresses, the Absolute. All change takes place within the Changeless. All form subsists within the Formless. All conditions obtain within that which is Limitless; and Creation is eternally going on within that which is Uncreated. All are activities of the One Mind and Spirit of God. All people come to a point of individuality within that which is Universal.

made. Even when it is pointed out that 'it is done unto us as we believe', we still remain rooted in what seems by far the greater reality — *conditions*. We fail to see how what we have been thinking about caused those conditions. We send more conditions after the conditions, seek solutions from the effects, of past thinking from thoughts already thought that have become conditions. It is as if we reshuffle a pack of cards endlessly, recombining them but never introducing a new element. To break into the new, we must start afresh from spirit, the formless principle of life from First Cause. We must initiate from our centre of creative authority: we must think a new thought, start a new train of causation.

Because the principle is not based on precedent, every association from our past that might cast a shadow over the present can be excluded as an influence. We take only the good from the past, let the rest go, proceed from a brand-new beginning. In this way, each and every day of our lives can be considered, and is, a new arrival at a new point, ever more productive, ever more enriching to our here-and-now experience.

'We do not have to create; all that we have to do is to think. Mind, the only mind that there is, creates.'

THE CREATIVE POWER OF THOUGHT

'As a man thinketh in his heart, so is he'. 'Nothing is, but thinking makes it so'. 'Thoughts are things'. How often have we heard these quoted, without feeling their reality. Emerson even went so far as to observe: 'Cannot hear what you say, for the shouting of what you are!'

Thought is the movement of consciousness. It works through law, but must be consciously directed. All thought takes definite form on the subconscious side of life. It is our thought, then, that 'shapes our lives'. What we are thinking, every moment, whether we are aware of it or not, is 'programming' our subconscious mind, which cannot help but act upon it, responding to it with matching conditions.

There are no exceptions. Thinking is not creative at one time and not another. There is no place to hide from it. Wherever we are, whatever we are doing, it is having an effect. We can distract ourselves, take long holidays, entirely ignore it; it will be working on, ceaselessly. In most forms of meditation the main goal is to arrest thought, stop it altogether to allow the experience of pure spirit. Even when this is achieved, thought takes up again, never having withdrawn as the active form of spirit. Always, what we outwardly are, and what we are to become, depends upon what we are thinking. This is the way we are using the creative intelligence of the universe, personally, at every breathing instant of our existence.

One analogy that illustrates this idea is to imagine that the universe is nothing but water, permeated by an infinite intelligence. Imagine that every time this intelligence moves, or thinks, ice is formed in the water, exactly corresponding to the thought. We might have countless pieces of ice of different form, colour and size, but these pieces of ice would still be water. If we could heat the entire mass, it would melt, and all forms would again become fluid. Nothing would have changed except form. The physical universe is spirit in form. Thought is an actual working power.

Once we see how our thought is forever creating our experience, we find ourselves on the horns of an unfamiliar dilemma. Do we push on, paying no attention to what now appears as the result of our thinking, attempt to write it off as 'coincidence' ('It would have happened anyway') — or, do we start to pay much stricter attention to what we are thinking and giving our attention without restraint or selectivity?

The choice is ours. There is no 'divine decree' that says how or what we should think. We have complete autonomy and freedom to think what we want to think. The only catch is this new perception: that there is a consequence of thought, that the same law that gives us all the good things of life — peace of mind, harmony, health, prosperity, fulfilment — can also bring sickness, misery, frustration, persistent mishaps and traumatic events — all according to what we have been giving priority in our thoughts.

This is the point at which we can either come to grips with this power within us that is ours to use, or try to forget about it, continue to 'muddle along' as we did before we ever heard about it or saw its possibilities. Most of us are used to the ups and downs, more comfortable with 'soldiering on', hoping for the best while expecting the worst, settling for half-measures, sharpening our defences, honing our cynicism with wit, compromise or wallowing in bitterness, anger, self-pity, blaming anyone or anything for the conditions of our lives other than ourselves. Blaming others is condoned, a game everyone is eligible to play with, perhaps, weather, physical ailments, taxes, the innate vileness of mankind as the chief targets.

In our negative views of life on earth, we are in a global unity. It is the common language that binds most of mankind in fellowship. 'Isn't it awful — isn't it shocking — well, what can you expect — it's just my luck — life's a . . .' Everyone understands everyone else at the negative level. It is only when thought becomes positive that one puts a curtain between oneself and the majority. One is accused of being a 'pollyanna', an 'idealist' and, perhaps worst indictment of all, 'a fool'.

Standing alone outside the crowd, moving against the herd, as positive thinkers, we must have a firmness of conviction that cannot be toppled by the onslaught of negativity that surrounds and engulfs us nor by disagreement nor even by pity. It is of no use to simply espouse a positive philosophy, repeat the most uplifting affirmations, if one does not have genuine understanding of why and how they work, the principle and law that underpins them. A superficial practice of positive thinking will prove itself fallible at the first great tragedy it confronts. True positive thinking will sustain us throughout any and every situation in our lives, no matter how dire.

Gaining any control of our 'destiny' — an ambiguous term in itself — necessarily involves, first, the acknowledgement of the power of our thought, the recognition of the precise effect of its law; second, the commitment, private and personal, to do the work of directing our thought. This work is the detection, denial and clearing out of our thinking of all that limits or blocks our good. We then need to replace it with thoughts that can only promote and ensure increase and improvement, not only for ourselves, but for all others we would like to support or help.

The wonder of the law of creative thinking is that the thoughts that may have done their damage when we were unaware can be brought into awareness and changed. What thought has done can be undone. A new way of thinking can be established at any time, simply by our decision. Old beliefs can be erased, neutralized, restated into law, they will then be responded to in the new way.

Negatives can thus be changed into positives. For example 'I don't like him' or 'I think she's jealous of me' can be changed to 'I don't like his behaviour, but I respect the divinity within him' or 'I see the fault may lie with me, and surround her with my love'. It may sound 'over the top', but if genuinely felt and meant — and *thought* — will have the effect of harmonizing our relationships. Of course, the same would apply to all situations and conditions of our lives.

Your thought is the creative spirit thinking in you, through you, as you. Its power is your power, when you know it is, and put it into action.

CONSCIOUS CONTROL OF YOUR THINKING

To gain any control of your thinking you must become more and more aware of its content. You are now a self-conscious unit of spirit, beyond the law of averages; what befalls the majority need not befall you. Once you have started to think with conscious intent, you can direct your thoughts in the way you want your life to go.

You can now dispel the belief that outer events rule you, or that unseen forces are at work at a subterranean level over which you have no possible means of defence. You are no longer at the mercy of the 'collective unconscious', the handing down of myths and legends and obsolete theories, or the 'brain-wash' of early conditioning, the expectations of parents, church or school. In fact, you will no longer allow any of your thinking to rest or simmer below the threshold of your *conscious* mind.

Your work now is to become as conscious of your thinking as possible. All your thoughts, not just some of them, all the time, not just occasionally, will now be fully employed in self-detection. You will examine your motives, explore *why* certain experiences that are taking place have come about. You will make every effort to recognize the reason why certain adverse conditions, difficult relationships, ill health have entered your life, instead of crediting them to unfortunate circumstances, other people's behaviour, or viruses that have chosen you to strike down. You will examine just what you have been thinking lately, or are carrying with you as a habit of your thought. You will reaffirm that everything in your life is there through consciousness, your consciousness. And everything that you do not want there can be cleared away by the same recognition.

It takes strength of resolve, and strong desire to give up being a prey to cliches, maxims which may not be so, 'common knowledge', 'common sense', human consensus, rules, traditions, manmade laws, and be under your own command. It also takes courage and daring to break out of doubt and be wholeheartedly aligned with your true identity, your God-self.

Above all, to bring your thoughts under conscious control requires skill, an art of thought in which the outer-directed, unordered, ambiguous blend of contradictory beliefs, interpretations and unacknowledged self-images is now brought to the surface, transposed from sub-conscious or unconscious to conscious, where it is dealt with by the *Self*.

In other words, the lower case self becomes capitalized; self-consciousness is now informed by Self-consciousness.

You have now arrived at the point of *Self-conscious living*. It is like getting into a car, automatically (sub-consciously) turning on the motor and setting it into motion, but then driving it where you want to go, by a chosen route: the car does not decide — you do. We teach the subconscious, learning first how to drive, then leave it to take over by its own law (as we do in walking, running, dressing, a vast list of actions that have become automatic or second nature.) The car is your means of getting where you want to go, as the body is the vehicle of your life experience, the brain the instrument of mind, the translator or transistor of spirit, universal intelligence, God — whatever concept suits you best.

In conscious living there is no further room for 'old wives' tales', superstitions, strange voices and visions, 'magic' black or white. There is no necessity for astrological charts, science fictional universes, governments of angels, dialogues with the discarnate.

Only that which is consciously directed can be certain of a desired result. To be sure that what is wanted, rather than what is not wanted, is manifested as experience, it must be consciously conceived and authorized. The Self is the authority to which the self gives voice.

With Self-directed living, we now become cognizant of the role of *choice* in gaining control of what 'happens' to us. To individualize itself for the purpose of expressing itself, creative intelligence or the infinite Self could not simply duplicate itself; that would be to create an automatic self pre-ordained to set conditions, robot-like, incapable of originating, developing, growing, progressing, led only by instinct, never to be the observer, the eyes and ears of God, the 'feedback' of an infinitely potential creator. The word 'individual', without the choice that leads to self-discovery, is a contradiction in terms. One cannot be automatic *and* individual.

Choice, therefore, is the pivotal factor in a self-controlled destiny, and this is the next focus of conscious attention. We begin to see and observe that everything is a question of choice. Choice begins from the moment we separate from the consciousness of our parents. Choice of what we will do, wear, eat, feel, begins from the moment we wake each day, is continuous and unremitting, whether or not we are aware of it: it is only through choice that we discover what works and what does not. If we continue to make the wrong choice, we continue to suffer its consequences. If we make a right choice, we see right action, find that right thinking equals right experience.

From this base it is imperative that we now make our choices consciously, choosing our thoughts with conscious care, as if we were crossing from one life-raft to another over a threatening sea.

One false step and we plunge into its amorphous depths, our survival once more relegated to randomness, out of our control.

When choice is consciously made, experience becomes Self-created. When it is left to the lower self, it is created from possible self-deception, self-delusion, self-imposed need for punishment or hurt, self-condemnation, the self-ishness of ego and insecurity, self-destructiveness in myriad forms.

When, however, choice is Self-chosen, it expresses as Self-fulfilment; self-assertion becomes Self-assertion. The former has fallible, questionable, mixed if not destructive results — the latter power for good. It is here that there must be a clear understanding and statement as to the nature of this Self — God, if you prefer. It can be stated in this way:

Spirit, God, Infinite Intelligence, the one and only Mind, is perfect, the only good, harmony, peace, abundance unlimited, love, joy, happiness. It knows nothing else. It gives you choice but knows nothing of what you have chosen that is unlike itself. So we say: what is true about Self is true about me: what is not true about Self (God) is not true about me.

And what is the truth, then? I am perfect, this is the one and only truth about me. The rest is falsehood, error, mistaken interpretation.

What we now need to do is to gain conviction of this, and to identify ever more closely with that which created us, to become it in this form of itself. Only with this identification can we achieve a level of confidence *based in identification with who we really are*. To become *all* that we really are must be our chief preoccupation. Over and over again we need to realize and accept that the infinite is for us, not against us. We do not need to fight any more, only trust and be thankful for the good that is ours for the acceptance.

Suppose that a parcel was delivered to you that needed your signature as receipt, and you said 'I don't want it'. It could not be forced upon you. That is like turning away your good. No gift must ever be rejected. All gifts come from the one giver, giving of itself through you.

This closing up of the distance between the self and the Self will also close the sense of separation between the impersonal and the personal. There can be a sense of companionship, of a constant friend, a meaningful communication that no longer depends on events and other people. This is true independence. It is not only *believing* in your worth and lovability, but *knowing* it.

As William James wrote: 'The religious man believes — the mystic knows.' You, we, all of us are incipient mystics. When we *know*, we are no longer incipient but realized.

78

9

TAKING CHARGE OF ONE'S OWN LIFE EXPERIENCE

Every seed must inevitably bring forth after its own kind, and thought is the seed of destiny.

Emmet Fox

It is now time to become specific. If in this world there were two doors, one marked 'All About God', and one marked 'God', the majority of mankind, including ourselves, would be streaming into the first, with only a relative trickle into the second. Almost everyone, with any interest whatever in the subject, is exhaustively preoccupied with the seeking of information on what can be done *for* them, not *by* them.

This is where, in the long view, 'the men become separated from the boys'. Here is where there is no way out or back. From here on, it is *do it yourself.*

Few take gladly to this dictum. It is severe, demanding, uncompromising. There is no built-in escape clause, no magic help or rescue, and so exacting it is that any self-deception is inescapably self-defeating. No one else but *you* can do with your consciousness what is needed to be done. *You* must make decisions; and *you*, alone, must take the responsibility for what happens to you from now on.

Taking the responsibility is, for most of us, the chief stumbling-block to moving on to freedom and growth. It means letting go of the past, with whatever injustice and pain it may have involved. It means forgiving the humanly unforgivable. It means releasing the hurtful and perhaps outrageous acts perpetrated on us in childhood, or the undeserved handicaps of physical defect, or even the 'karmic' effects, if that is what we believe, that have expressed themselves in the circumstances of our birth and background in this life — all without redress.

Unconsciously, for the most part, we will not settle without redress. We want the score settled; we want people to understand what they have done to us, to pay for it, suffer for it. Only if we feel we may have brought a penalty with us from a previous life is responsibility for our own experience acceptable without redress.

We may undergo hypnotherapy to find this out, and still not be able to deal with it: for ultimately, one way or the other, there is no alternative to assuming responsibility for our own lives. It is the one and only way to be free to grow. And we can be sure that life, infinite intelligence itself, will do a far more effective job of redress than we can, for every real intention or motive precisely manifests itself, not as punishment but as inevitable consequence.

To bolster a decision to let go of the past, it helps to know that everybody does the best they can at any particular stage of their lives. Ignorance of the law may not excuse those who have 'sinned' against you, but if they had known better, they would have done better. It is extremely rare that anyone does anything to us with *malicious* intent, including you.

Unconscious resistance to responsibility, however, has baffled even the most ardently desirous of resolution and self-emergence. It is stealthily interwoven in our life-conditioning that blame is to be laid on the outside, not on ourselves. It is easier than reciting the alphabet to say what caused this or that to happen to us. The finger of blame can be pointed at every person with whom we have ever been involved, at every level: the government, the neighbours, the city, state, town, village or street, the institutions, the weather, the ruthless indifference of natural laws. It is considered normal, and wins sympathy without explanation when we blame life for all our misfortunes. When good things happen, we are more apt to assume we have 'done something right' — yet here, too, it is often ascribed to 'good luck'.

Luck engenders more belief than any inner principle of thought, any connection with the effect of our thinking. Our greatest gift to others is our 'wish' for them to have good luck. 'Good luck' means hoping we will be lucky, that 'fortune' will 'smile' on our efforts, that we will win a gamble that will lift our lives out of an otherwise unalterable rut. It so seasons our language that it is generally assumed to be a more valid and reliable fact of life than any other, particularly reliance on 'God's will', which, it is suspected, may or may not be on our side, or in time to save the day.

If luck is still believed in more than the nature and quality of one's thinking, then responsibility is still, if only unconsciously, deferred. True understanding, together with complete acceptance of the basic principle being dealt with, cannot co-exist with fragments of contradictory beliefs.

When the authority of your own conviction is given over to the authority of other people's beliefs, *they* are the rulers of your destiny, not *you*. If you still believe that outer conditions are to be blamed for your experience, and that luck plays a major role in the daily events of your life, then you are still in the thrall of old effects, old thoughts, which are like a wake following the tide, like yesterday's news, like the echo of bells that were rung last week, year or decade.

'But,' many people will say, with scepticism, even bitterness, 'how can you say that I caused myself all this trouble when I make every effort to help myself, explore every opportunity, work hard, apply myself diligently to whatever is required of me, serve others, sacrifice my own comfort to do good? How can you say that I brought on this cold, this illness, this accident, this change in government policy, this change of heart in the one I love, this loss of friendship, this disappointment in my ambitions, this loss of a beloved?'

Yes, it may seem beyond belief — but the only absolute certainty of our lives is that we really do bring on these experiences ourselves. However, once we can do our own thinking, once we have become conscious that we are thinking beings, that thought is an energy that corresponds if directed with definite purpose, then the results will prove this truth. This is why it can be called a science of thought, for even if in the least degree, it is no longer a hypothesis but a verifiable and repeatable proof.

As to what happens to us *before* we are conscious of ourselves and the power of our thought, when we are still in the keeping and power of others, as in infancy and early childhood, the same cannot be said. It would behoove us to dredge up from buried childhood wounds an awareness that can now be handled with conscious thinking and finally released. Even the worst case of child abuse, for instance, must eventually be relegated to a past that has gone forever. No river flows backward, but ever moves on. Similarly, your life is impelled forward to the ever new, the *now* you. To retain the good from all that has flowed behind you is practical and wise — for there have been in everyone's life, no matter how troubled, moments of contentment, harmony, joy, even if so brief as to have been almost forgotten. Full responsibility for one's life must contain a balance. One should not 'throw the baby out with the bathwater' in one's zeal for taking authority.

A full, honest recognition of as much as is possible to us in a clear and contemplative frame of mind needs always to be present, as we make the attempt to assume the power of our own word. It benefits us little if we think one way one hour and another the next. What is the subconscious to make of such mixed directives? 'I want a new job in another country', might be a clear-cut declaration at one moment, but in the next 'I would like a new house in town' might be felt in your consciousness, setting up an undertow of conflict. The new job could be what you think you *should* want, while your heart is not really in the move. The result will seem like the law not working to demonstrate what you want to experience, but even when the law appears not to be working, it is working by not working — for you have programmed it with disbelief.

The thoughts that we have during the course of a waking day contain so many contradictions, are so diverse, mercurial, confused, that it is a wonder we can use them with as much effect as we do, without even trying. In Eastern philosophy, the incredible range of our thoughts is sometimes referred to as 'the monkey mind'. In modern biofeedback terminology it is called 'cocktail chatter' — the state that precedes the brain waves settling down before the 'fifth state' of calm thoughtlessness, as in meditation.

Thoughts can leap from one subject to another, have a dialogue with invisible people, write an articulate letter or shopping list, decide what to wear or eat, sing an old song, travel back to childhood or round the world, mutter hostile comments about a relative or employer, outline a stratagem for world peace, acknowledge various discomforts or suspicious feelings in the body, feel euphoric hope for an ambitious dream.

The reason for this limitless range is that the nature of thought is associative; one thought leads to another in an endless linkage of sense and suggestion. A glimpse in a lighted window, a sniff of some remembered perfume, a certain laugh, a burst of birdsong, the echo of a lowing cow, a train whistle in the night, even the reflected image of our own face in the mirror can carry us off and away without conscious awareness.

How, then, can one ever gain control of one's thinking? Is it really possible — or is it just a very good idea, one we might all aspire to, but without much hope of success?

The answer is that it is possible. It may take time — but what else is there? What alternative — that we have so far heard of or know about — is there?

In the words of Roger Walsh, we are privileged to have the opportunity. He writes:

We are called to a task greater than that demanded of any generation in human history: to preserve our planet and our species. In accepting this challenge we are also called to recognize, develop and redirect the awesome power of our minds, and to consciously choose and create our evolution.

Never in the course of human history have so many people needlessly suffered and died. Never in the course of human history have so many hungered and been oppressed. And never have so many lives (some five billion) hung in the balance.

And never in the course of human history have the opportunities been greater. Never have we had such powerful resources and technologies available to relieve world suffering. Never has there been such a potential for developing a global psychology to understand the motives and behaviours that threaten us, and those that may yet save us. The magnitude of our difficulties may be matched only by the magnitude of our opportunities...There is exciting and desperately needed work to be done.

The point is, for those of us who want to do this work and take this opportunity, it is best accomplished by individual conscious choice, so that the results emanate and radiate from within us rather than being inflicted or enforced by outer rule. We do not have the need to run away from any outer reality: we need to confront the inner reality, and by our inspired poise and Self-confidence cause changes to take place in the world at large.

Immanuel Kant said, 'Act always so that the immediate motive of thy will may become a universal rule for all intelligent beings.' And thousands of years ago the Buddha said: 'We are what we think. All that we are arises with our thoughts. With our thoughts we make the world.'

As for overcoming whatever reservations one might still hold against final surrender, Henry Ford wryly commented: 'Those who believe they can do something, and those who believe they can't, are both right.'

On the other hand — there is the advice of Johann Wolfgang von Goethe: 'Whatever you can do, or dream you can, begin it. Boldness has genius, power and magic in it.'

HOW TO DO IT — SOME TECHNIQUES OF TAKING CHARGE

To make full and constructive use of the axiom 'Thoughts are things', requires that you come to realize that there is a power in the universe greater than you are, and you can use it...So, if you find that your life is not all that you would have it be, it becomes necessary to change your patterns of thinking. You need to uproot those undesirable thoughts you have planted and replace them with others more to your liking.

Willis Kinnear

Since most of the damage that we do to our personal lives stems from a strongly ingrained habit of negative thinking — that is, the conditioned tendency to take a generally dim view of human existence (a view shared by the majority of mankind) — the first place to start reshaping your life for the better is to begin eliminating negative thought patterns, uprooting them as completely as possible, and replacing them with positive ones. Although not as easily done as said, this is nevertheless the primary requirement of a self-controlled experience in which the potential of normal happiness can be realized.

The insidious habit of negative thinking is interlaced so tightly through the substance of our consciousness that it is seldom even noticed. Not until it is pointed out to us do we begin to hear ourselves giving voice to it in the negative observations we make, the negative attitudes we express. The first reaction to the discovery is to deny it — usually vehemently, proclaiming that we are quite the opposite, optimistic and hopeful — within reason. One must, after all, be *realistic*. If, however, the habit is not too compulsive and deep-seated, work to remove it can begin. A spring-cleaning of all its effects can free the consciousness, make space for renewal in the positive.

In the process we may become uncomfortably aware of the negativity of others, particularly those closest to us, and of almost everyone with whom we are involved, bombarded by the negative opinions of 'experts' in every aspect of current affairs, the chaos, horror and confusion. Much effort is needed to weed a garden where the long established weeds continue to choke out the newly planted flowers.

Yet the ability to withstand the onslaught of negativity is essential to anyone wanting to gain control of experience. One can no longer 'afford' to waver or regress: once one has seen the proof of what every thought does, it is simply asking for negative experience. Also small, seemingly trivial negatives, such as 'dirging' about transport, weather, lack of parking spaces, noise and fumes, the inconsiderateness of people, rises in cost, and a miscellany of anxieties that sneak in the side door of your thinking may accumulate, gather shape and force and result in a so-called 'accident' — such as not quite making a jump onto a bus, with resultant injury.

Similarly, grumbling away under one's breath may so put one out of harmony that one hits one's head on a cupboard door, burns one's hand on the stove, bangs one's shins against a post. The subconscious did not know these negatives were not meant or should not be recorded — it was itself, a law at work, responding to what was given it by means of thought. A small negative, an accumulation of negatives, a very large and intensely felt negative — these are all the same to the law.

The important message for you, for all of us, is to be totally aware of what we are doing to ourselves and our lives with our every thought. It makes no difference what other people are thinking. You cannot be responsible for their negativity. They are building their experience, you are building yours — and this, though you can do it the moment you decide to, is not a part-time work, but a full-time, lifelong project.

To be utterly practical about it, you need to apply some techniques, which, while sounding a bit foolish, are instantly effective. For example: with your new-found awareness of the powerful habit of a negative commentary going on in your mind, every time you hear a negative observation or statement begin, do not let it complete itself — say something like this — 'cancel, cancel'. Say it forcefully.

Additionally: imagine a blackboard, a slate, on which the negative thought is forming. Take a large eraser and wipe it off before it can be finished. Do it again, and yet again if it still insists on forming, until it has completely vanished.

Another useful device is to visualize a large pair of shears. Cut the negative in half, firmly, with one big sharp movement that does not allow it to piece together again.

Amusing, perhaps, but effective, is to imagine a little blind in your forehead which, when you or someone else makes a negative statement, comes rapidly down with a sign on it saying 'out to lunch'. You may then continue to smile at the other person, who will not be aware that you are not agreeing or affected, and you will not have imposed on them your ideas or belief. By the time you 'get back from lunch' you will have omitted registering your negative.

Of more frequent and daily use is the statement, made to yourself while others or you are offering by-now familiar negative 'wisdom', that 'There is not a word of truth in it. It is neither person, place nor thing. It has no validity in law, is no part of infinite intelligence, and therefore has no grip or hold on me'. Steady practice of this technique of denial will find its support in the subconscious law and the negative result will be dissolved before it can be 'programmed'.

The subconscious mind has been likened to a computer, into which our thoughts, deliberately or otherwise fed, are given back in exact results. This analogy is graphic, but limited. The computer has no intelligence of its own: we have fed it ours. The subconscious mind has infinite intelligence. In the same way as the computer, it must accept the data given it, cannot refuse or reject, but with this great difference: the 'bio-computer' has the creative medium of the universe to work with. It may not ask 'why', but it knows *how* — to do anything. Whatever the universe is composed of, out of this initiating substance, it can immediately go to work to manifest it in like kind.

Another great difference is that it never rests: our thoughts are received in it at all times under all conditions, from everywhere, far beyond our terms and conceptions of time, or distance. That is why it is said to be 'a blind force', 'servant of the spirit' — never knowing why, only doing.

It is awesome to contemplate that with this great power that is ours to command and direct, there can be no such thing as the impossible. As a business slogan comments: 'The impossible may take a bit longer.' Even this we must deny — for if we say to the subconscious, 'This will take a bit longer', then, of course, you have programmed it to take a bit longer, and it *will*.

Having discussed to some small extent the insidiousness of 'the dim view' of the way the world and human nature 'is', it becomes necessary to consider the opposite — the *positive* viewpoint. Can it be cultivated to take over our thinking so as to point our lives in a more satisfactory direction?

It not only can, but will, and does so from the moment we start to adopt it consciously and deliberately, with real understanding of why we are doing so, why it works, the principle behind it. To simply recite and repeat positive statements, which is something of a current fashion in 'pop' psychology, may be of some benefit — certainly a step up from the infectious disease of negativity. However, this is not a method to rely on, being always fallible and vulnerable to collapse when confronted with dire crises.

To achieve genuine, durable results, positive thinking needs to be rooted in the conviction that our thinking is a law to itself, that we are not just separate, floating entities having to make it completely on our own, pull ourselves up by our own 'bootstraps'. On the contrary, we are inseparably connected to a higher power, an intelligence that is *infallible*, with which we can identify, and which by its nature is and can only consist of all that is positive. Being omnipotent, it knows nothing of anything else but the positive.

The art of positive thinking, therefore, is the art of making this connection and this *identification*. Starting as an exercise, it gradually becomes second nature, and when this happens there are few situations or conditions in life that cannot be directed for the better.

It brings increased competence at the human level, increased energy, improved health, less necessity for those substitutive efforts of human willpower such as tenacity, fortitude, resourcefulness and resilience — all very commendable in themselves, but ultimately exhausting and often abortive. Replaced by trust, true confidence in who one is and by what power one is supported, this unremitting effort is given over to increased perceptions and insights. The deepening of spiritual will, which is never forced, unfolds itself as more 'light' by which to 'see', to 'know'. This now comes without strain, with patience for what you do not yet know. In the never-ending process of inner learning, your mistakes are now acknowledged without self-condemnation. There is only a 'divine discontent' that urges you on, never to find a plateau where there is no more to know.

The suggestion, as with the techniques for dealing with negative thinking, is to start with a simple, basic procedure: every time you make a negative statement or observation, or have a negative feeling or attitude, you should instantaneously *reverse* it — to a positive one.

For instance: 'I don't like or trust him, he's got shifty eyes' turns into, 'However he looks, he is divinely created, is probably lost and afraid. May he find his way and his good'. Someone has grabbed your seat or jumped the queue in front of you. Waves of anger, resentment, even hate fill you with negative eloquence. You stop, catch yourself and say, 'Such need to push and grab from others is terrible insecurity. It is stupid to resent them for it.'

Perhaps someone in your office, or in your home, has hurt your feelings with an unfair criticism. The bitterness you feel may lead you to mutter one adamant negative statement after another, destroying your appetite, your health, your sleep. Examine what has been said or done. Say, 'I understand why they might have felt this way and said what they did. They were not being aware that in hurting me they were hurting themselves. If they had known better they would not have acted in this way. The law of compensation will take its effect. I release my anger and my hurt, knowing that no one can hurt me or run my mind unless I let them, and the infinite never rejects its own, only I can reject myself — which I now refuse to do.'

With this reversal of feeling a sense of harmony and peace moves over your negative atmosphere, eliminating it. Practised consistently, the habit of negative thinking is replaced with the habit of positive thinking. The habit takes over, just as the negativity did before.

The exercise of reversing can be applied to any and all situations, not necessarily in line with those given above. Sometimes you may use it for trivial happenings, sometimes for large issues. You need to take it with you wherever you go, whatever you are doing, giving it the same persistence that you previously gave to your negative efforts.

It is, however, a safe assumption that positive thinking is much, much harder to establish than it at first appears. The tendency to lapse, to fall back into the easy, familiar terms of a negative outlook or expectation, is like putting on old slippers or broken-shoes — comfortable, almost comforting. Many people speak of the relief of giving up trying to be positive and just indulging with abandon in the darkest of thoughts. Even knowing the consequence, the temptation is often irresistible.

Once the proof has been seen, the indulgence is more and more feared, and avoided: it is simply not worth it. It is like deciding on abandoning a diet for an orgy of rich food and drink — you pay for it the next day.

There can be such a thing as fear of negativity, becoming afraid of one's own thoughts, that they cannot be controlled. Fear of outer things may become fear of one's own mind. Even so, there is no way to turn back on the knowledge that each thought must count. If your every thought were to be recorded on tape, then played back at full volume for all to hear, their exposure would undoubtedly embarrass if not appal you. Few of us would want others to know what we are *really* feeling, *really* thinking; what we really think is seldom acceptable in the context of society. Many of us would have no friends, or lose the ones we had, if we did not edit and censor our thoughts before we expressed them. We would acquire little prestige, be unable to maintain façades, tell white lies, guard or bolster our egos, impress our students or colleagues

or employers, convince our children, our bank managers, or produce excuses for our inadequacies. We might still befuddle our
psychiatrists with deceits and half-truths, be relatively at ease with
loving, open-minded parents or relatives, but possibly only be
quite safe with our animals, who will accept and love us without
question or judgement.

The successful practice of conscious thinking is most often
blocked by the lack of conviction.

What we think does matter. It matters so much, in fact, that it
can be said that there is nothing else *but* thinking — and what
it does. To absorb this truth opens out the way for control.

A good exercise to prove this to yourself is to try an experiment
with your thinking. For one week, if you can bear to, allow yourself to think negatively about anything and everything. The
weather is always a good place to start: 'What a nasty day. The
cold will probably keep up for the rest of the spring, kill off the
buds. Remember that blizzard last year.' Then there's the traffic,
yesterday's bomb, a death or plane crash that can set the tone.
Just keep it going, without censorship.

At the end of the week, look to the conditions of your life. Assess
them. Instead of 'It was not my day', or 'One thing led to the other
in ways you wouldn't believe', connect them to what you allowed
yourself to be thinking. Do not exclude ailments and physical mishaps, note the way in which they have become translated into
outer conditions. Do not write them off as accidental or coinciden-
tal or caused by other people.

Now take another week and practise 'reversing' the negatives,
erasing them with the techniques suggested, making positive
statements, acting with faith and optimism, giving others the right
to their divinity, minding your own business not theirs, expecting the best, doing the most you can with each day to the utmost
of your ability with a whole heart. Again, at the end of the week
assess the conditions of your life, the quality of your experience.
The difference should be distinctly apparent in a general uplift
and improvement of your experience, with some manifestations
seeming almost 'too good to be true'.

Only you will recognize whether or not your experiment has
been successful, a proof of the principle. You may share it verbally with others, but they may fail to be impressed. You are the
one who must be impressed — impressed enough to make conscious thinking your central concern.

There can be, for many, a great difficulty in maintaining a positive flow, keeping out the flow of negatives. There is a small book-
let called 'The 7-Day Mental Diet', by Emmet Fox, in which he

advocates keeping negative thoughts out of consciousness as far as possible for seven days. At the end of that time our thoughts should have changed so much, that we will never be the same. It is well known to those many thousands who have tried 'the diet' that it is close to impossible to keep the negative thoughts from forming for 24 hours, let alone seven days.

Advocated here is to do as the AA (Alcoholics Anonymous) recommends with taking an alcoholic drink: take it one day at a time. Say 'I have only to abstain this day'. The next day, of course, you do the same, until the days mount up — and there you are, relatively free.

Another method is to attempt a 'balance of power': to see a pair of scales in your mind, your negative thoughts going onto one side of the scales, your positive thoughts going onto the other. If you can put the first 51 per cent onto the positive side, you have begun to tilt the balance of power. From here, by extending the amount of time each day that you think on the positive side, your positive thoughts will gain ascendancy and finally give you control of the quality of your experience.

The vigilance required firstly to detect the trend of our thinking, and secondly to bring it into line is apt to be lost in a very busy, outwardly oriented consciousness. Thoughts become drowned in physical action, and in mental preoccupation with the world of the already thought, the world of effects that we have already built and are now living through. To offset this strong tendency to forget, to be led away from our conscious hold before we have it established, it is crucial to start each day in full cognizance, to launch it, so to speak, before we plunge into the outer world. In this way, we consciously take charge and establish the principle for outer events to follow.

To give a very concrete example: often when getting up in the morning, we start a downward trend of mood and thought, and by the time we have had breakfast we have established an anxious, grim approach to the day. It is vital that before this can happen we should firmly remind ourselves of who we really are, what wonderful opportunities life holds for us if we take them and do not extinguish their power with *self*-imposed limitations. Instead of allowing the shadows of gloom, we should command them to go, and give to our subconscious law the order of what we *do* want of this day.

For instance, instead of thinking, 'Oh Lord, I'm really not looking forward to today', or 'I don't feel up to it and wish I could just stay home, or take off for a holiday,' we might say:

Today is the happiest, most fulfilling, most productive, most

joyous day of my entire life. It starts right now — and I give thanks for it. And so it *is*!

This could, of course, be used as an 'any day' calendar. It will always apply, but the wording may be more personal to each of us. If it sounds excessive to those who do not understand the basis from which it draws expression, it will become an understatement to you, who every day are more closely identified with the source of your authority.

In other words, authorize your day. Take charge of it. Decide how it shall be in your own terms. Do not let it drift and take you along with it into the random effects of your undirected thinking. Do this each morning — and then do the same thing, as much as you can, during the rest of your waking day. Speak with the same authority before you go to sleep, and even your dreams will reflect a happier order than if you just sink unprepared, unprogrammed into the universal subconscious where your personal point of contact with it is, metaphorically, 'on hold'.

Be very wary of 'mixed' or contradictory directives. Always be clear as to what you really want to experience. Knowing what you want may be the most elusive area of your conscious thinking. Most of us do not know what we really want. We may believe we do, but it may be made up of what we 'should' want, what will please others, or placate, win the approval of some human authority in our lives. Too often, albeit unconsciously, we will rule out what we really want in life as selfish, over-ambitious, undeserved, unrealistic. We may feel guilty in wanting a happy or prosperous life while there is so much suffering in the world, so many people going without the barest necessities. We may feel too beholden to others to even consider enjoying a self-chosen life. We tie ourselves to our unconscious beliefs, and often to our own prejudices, obscuring the potential available to us. God does not ordain us to deny our own self-expression. God does not ordain that we should limit our lives. There is only one law, a price to pay for wrong choices, a law that exacts the 'uttermost farthing' if what we do harms others or goes against the harmony of universal order, but which equally responds in kind to right thought and right action.

So in trying to clarify what we *do* want from life, as opposed to what we do *not*, it is uncalled for to modify, curtail, mitigate the *ideally* wanted. We need not say, 'It was meant' or 'not meant to be' — that is fatalistic, implying a pre-ordained plan we cannot escape, an absence of choice and 'free will'. God, or spirit, or infinite life, has only one plan — and that is for fuller and fuller expression, growth, unfoldment of itself, its own creation, its own forms.

Conscious thinking entails that we, ourselves, take the reins, direct the law that cannot direct itself but only respond. Even when we say 'I transfer my burden', 'Over to you, God' , or the much repeated and sometimes glib 'Let go — let God,' we are not placing the *responsibility* onto God, but onto our own trust in an immutable law.

This is why healing takes place, and why anything can be healed, in mind or body, or both — because we allow the truth about us to be revealed. It was always there. It was mostly a disbelief in the perfection of spirit or God that prevented the healing. One of the most difficult concepts of all in the adoption of conscious thinking is this concept of our own perfection. That we are already perfect — not becoming perfect, but unfolding perfection, a perfect idea, is a new and unfamiliar view. Mind can only be perfect, and the ingredients of this perfection — love, beauty, peace, wisdom, goodness, harmony, health, joy — are its sole ingredients. It neither contains nor knows of any other. This requires deeper understanding of a spiritual life principle.

It is only because we have been given choice as the means of individualizing and discovering ourselves that we see ingredients of an opposite nature. It is we who invented the opposites, the 'devil', to give name to our doubts and misinterpretations. We see evil as a force in itself, because of our ignorance of the whole.

It is open to us, in conscious thinking, to begin to align ourselves with the perfect, to disown the imperfect as ignorance in transit. Consciously, we sense this as the truth, declare it, and in the declaration set the law of mental equivalents into motion.

In conscious thinking, we must have the mental equivalent of that which we want to experience. We cannot experience more than the mental equivalent we can provide. To give a crude analogy, if we want a Jaguar but all we can genuinely conceive of ourselves as having is a Ford, it is unlikely that we will make manifest a Jaguar in our experience. 'The subconscious cannot be fooled' is a conscious thinking maxim. The subconscious will pick up our unconscious reservations and reflect them as failure, but in reality be a precise match of the embodiment within the declarer's consciousness.

It is right and good the the law works so reliably, for this is also our opportunity to expand and rise out of all previous conditions. Raise the mental equivalent, believe in it, and nothing can hinder its manifestation.

The next facet of conscious thinking is that of genuine acceptance. Receptivity and acceptance of our good is a prerequisite of controlled experience. We can know what we want, and still not accept it, and there is absolutely nothing the law can do to give it to us. If we will not receive, spirit cannot force it on us. We usually interpret this as a failed demonstration. The kingdom may be waiting for us, but we cannot inherit it if we do not claim it.

Conscious thinking lays claim. It 'seeks first the kingdom', and sees that 'all else is given unto you' is proven. In conscious thinking you do not have to have all the answers, to know all of God. You do not have to satisfy sharp interrogation or mass world opinion. You do not have to acquit yourself as a great samaritan, hero or heroine, or missionary. You have only one thing to prove — yourself to yourself, the integrity of your own thoughts, the actualization of your spiritual self. As Robert Browning wrote so wisely:

> Truth is within ourselves; it takes no rise
> From outward things, whate'er you may believe.
> There is an inmost centre in us all,
> Where truth abides in fullness; and to KNOW
> Rather consists in opening out a way
> Whence the imprisoned splendour may escape,
> Than in effecting entry for a light
> Supposed to be without.

CONSCIOUS DECLARATION

What good is the possibility until it is used? What good is knowledge unless we make practical application of it? Therefore we must definitely speak our conviction in concrete form in Mind.

Ernest Holmes

This, in essence, describes the objective of conscious declaration. It is a definite statement spoken with the authority of the one and only creative power, a specific directive to subconscious law. Unlike orthodox prayer which supplicates, makes promises, bargains, attempts to win merit, or says, 'if it's all right with you, God,' it assumes identification and unification with the original source of all life.

Conscious declarations are made for the declarer or for another, for limitless needs, goals, desires, but always with the absolute conviction of their truth, never to manipulate or harm or for any purpose other than the increase of good and happiness for oneself and all.

Once made and set in motion, a conscious declaration can be considered already achieved. The only way in which it could fail to manifest would be a contradiction of directive, a change of heart, or a too automatic, 'Well, I certainly *hope* it is so!' Hope places it in question — it may, or may not be going to work! Conscious declaration is an edict not only assuming rule but commanding it — a command the subconscious cannot help but 'demonstrate' in kind.

Taking conscious command, therefore, is the main work toward the control of individual experience. There is no element of coercion, rather the calm, sure acceptance of *knowing* with what limitless power one is dealing. In conscious thinking, you learn to play your life from a position of unshakable strength, dependent on no thing or person or condition other than spirit, God, omnipotent creative intelligence.

It should be noted that there is nothing totally new about this procedure: close communion with a power greater than individual man has laced our history, taken too many forms to enumerate, and even here is but a synthesis in concept, except for the one, unique element — Self-assertion.

All other forms of communication with the 'godhead' place its created beings in a secondary role, at most as participants in their creation. No other belief system tells it what to do, commandeers its power. As a 'way', there is nothing 'holy' about conscious direction, it is not sacramental or doctrinal, creates, yet within its own right of consciousness.

Having a 'say' is an act of conscious declaration. The 'say' is the voice of the transient form of the formless absolute, the listener, and the listened to are one and the same but for degree.

Additionally, there is no limit to what can be consciously declared. There is no more practical means of directing the conditions of your experience. It is manifestly true that you *can* 'create your own tomorrow'. All that can hold up the process is failure to put it into practice.

Practice, practice, practice. This is the fuse of power behind self-applied direction. Intellectual grasp is essential, but can only lead you to the gateway of your potential. It is better to have a tiny portion of actual practice, actual declaring, backed by feeling, than all the theory there is, no matter how well understood.

How, in the light of this practical approach to the control of your experience should you set about it? What form should a 'declaration' take? Is there any one particular structure? How long or short should it be? How often does it need to be made, and does it need to be repeated? Is there a special 'feeling' that goes with it? For whom apart from oneself, can one declare for? Do we need to ask, or can we volunteer declarations for anyone we feel needs one?

All these questions and more need to be answered with care. It is patently true, for example, that many people who are unhappy or unwell do not really want to recover; their troubles or ailments may be their only claim to attention, interest and control of others. For many of us, to be free of complaints is to risk being dull and even boring; conversations can come to a dead halt with 'I'm fine, thank you'. *Any* ailment or complication may be preferable to none. (It can be more politic to claim one, while repeating to yourself, 'There's not a word of truth in it!' and forgive yourself for engendering sympathy.)

It is, therefore, wise to refrain from declaration where healing may be unconsciously resisted; there are enough troubled people in the world who desperately need help, without going looking for them. So it is better to wait to be asked, but once asked, a declaration must be scupulously honoured.

To return to the previous questions, however, the answer to the first three can be combined:

1.   You should just start right where you are in your understanding — 'plunge in', so to speak. It does not matter whether you are sitting, standing, lying, walking along the street, just so long as you can 'tune out' any distractions and still yourself, centre your attention. Do not let noise bother you, or set up any elaborate conditions to induce a 'right mood'. You should be able to make a conscious declaration at any time or in any place where you happen to be.

2.   The declaration does not need a permanent form or structure, except when you first begin its practice. It is like learning to play the piano by doing basic exercises, gradually enlarging their range and becoming familiar with the keyboard, until the familiarity allows you to make an infinite variety of chords and harmonies. The original exercises are not abandoned or forgotten, but are incorporated into the free use of the instrument.

So in the beginning, the following structure is suggested — bearing in mind that the chief aim of conscious declaration is to separate false beliefs from the truth as you believe it; to adhere to the principle that what is true of God is true to you, and what is not true of God is not true of you — and to uncover and reveal rather than to establish this truth. Towards this end six basic steps form a useful guide:

95

1   Recognition

Here you define the nature of God. Make statements about what you believe God to be in your own terms. You might think up a list of synonyms, such as infinite love, infinite good, perfect spirit, the one mind, life-force or essence of being. Try to enlarge your vocabulary for this concept and become easy and familiar with it. Develop a 'flow', silently or audibly, whichever gives you the greater sense of energy and conviction. You might focus your belief with comments such as 'Through my mind God thinks. Through my heart God expresses divine love. Through my body God expresses perfect life, health and vitality.' (Substitute 'it' for God or 'his' if this causes resistance.) 'There is no life, truth, substance or intelligence in evil; God, the good, is all there really is, and I am surrounded and filled with it. In my life God is the only activity now taking place. I have spiritual wisdom, spiritual perception and spiritual discernment. I love truth, speak truth, rejoice in truth, for God is truth.'

2   Self-Definition

You now begin to affirm the spiritual reality of man. Just as you have made a series of statements about yourself as part of the omnipotent creator, you now name all that you can know about your spiritual possibilities. All the attributes you have given God can now be given to yourself. Do this daily until it becomes easy. You are clearing up your own ideas about yourself. You can sum it all up in a comment such as 'God acts through me, as me, in me, and all life.'

3   Denial and Affirmation

In this step there is a choice to make. It is between the 'argumentative' method, and the 'affirmative' method. In the argumentative method you define what is troubling you or blocking your good, and by restatement of the basic principle convince yourself that whatever it is, there is no possible truth in it, no valid law to support it, and that its false interpretations of reality are now entirely released from your consciousness. This is followed by affirmation of what is true.

In the affirmative method you do not deny, but go straight to the affirmation of the basic principle. This is a procedure that suits those who do not want to give importance to what is wrong, who would rather put their thought-energy into what is right, positive, perfect.

96

There is, however, a need for individual assessment of which method is preferable. If, for instance, there is an excessive state of fear, anxiety, stress or frustration, a desire persistently blocked, then it might be crucial to work through the denial. It serves no purpose to *say* there is only good and all is well, when you are being pulled by opposite feelings into not *believing* it because you have only repressed rather than brought out and dealt with the non-truth. If, on the other hand, it simply makes more trouble for you, and you can do without the denial, then it would be a wiser choice for you to use the affirmative method. Only be sure that your affirmation is not superficial, not merely recited words learned by heart, but is based in spirit and in truth, backed by belief and conviction.

4 Unification

Here you should create a deep sense of your oneness with that which created you. You attempt to eliminate the word 'and' from your thoughts and vocabulary and to substitute the word 'as'. Say to yourself, in conscious awareness of what it means, that it is not God *and* man, but God *as* man that is the truth of life. *You*, therefore, are not the whole *and* the part, but the whole *as* the part. You affirm that there is and can be no separation, that you are always inseparably unified with the power of universal intelligence. In fact, there is really no process of unification, there is only *at-one-ment*, here, now, eternally. And so, added to unification is — realization. You are Self-realized.

5 Declaration

This is the central step in all conscious authority. Here is where you become specific in your statements, exact in your directives, where your Self takes command of your self without any further deference to any form of human psychology, no matter how knowledgeable. It also leaves all forms of medical interpretation behind to become a psychology of the spirit, a healer by means of spirit.

To make a conscious declaration is to make a pronouncement, based in total faith — faith, here, being an operative term, not a theological mandate. Faith in this context is the bow to the arrow, trigger to the explosive, lift-off to flight, the propelling force of the invisible into the visible, the unmanifest into the manifest.

You make a conscious declaration in complete trust that it must take form, according to its specification. The specification has no superimposed limit if it can answer these questions: Do the things we want lend themselves to a constructive, fulfilling, more abundant life? Do they rob no one, hurt no one, and express a greater degree of livingness? If we are able to answer these questions affirmatively, then all the power in the universe is behind us in beneficent support.

As Ernest Holmes has written: 'We are not dependent upon chance but upon the Law. The responsibility of setting the Law in motion is ours, but the responsibility of making it work is inherent in its own nature.'

Here is one example of a *conscious declaration* that can be applied for general 'right action' (Individual declarations for specific symptoms, needs and desires are given later).

> I now take authority over my life. Living consciously under the Law of Mind is within my power, for I have the gift of choice. The Law of infinite intelligence that receives the patterns of my thoughts and feelings and acts to bring them into manifest form, always responds to me. I live my life effectively, energetically and vigorously now. I take dominion over my own life from my inner Self. I choose my responses consciously and live deeply in the life of spirit. I attain fuller freedom of self-expression by being alert and aware of what I am thinking and feeling each moment. As I observe my inner and outer reactions, without critical judgement, a hidden conditioning under which I have unconsciously lived is revealed. As the patterns become apparent, I move to appropriate and beneficial responses. Any unwanted patterns and effects are replaced with wholesome, healthy, positive expressions. Knowing that infinite intelligence is continually available to me for insight and decision, I live more consistently in faith, peace, love and joy. I am ever more calm, kind and creative. In this loving awareness, I meet the good I desire, and I achieve ever greater, more soul-satisfying mastery in my life.

6 Release into Law

This, the last step, consists of letting go all traces of doubt or uncertainty that may linger beneath the threshold of your consciousness. It is surrender to trust, a total dedication in heart and mind to acceptance, appreciation and thankfulness for what you know is already accomplished. There is no further need for you to dig up the roots to see if the plant of your desire is growing. You know that it is. You do not have to look. You now act and feel as if it is already in blossom. Your dreams of good are not *going* to come true, they are already true and have only to be welcomed.

Words of praise and gratitude will set a seal on your release. Assured, free of question, you have empowered the law to positive action, have set the law of attraction into unobstructed reflection. There is nothing more for you to do, nothing more you can do, except, perhaps, to say 'It is done. I accept. I believe. I *know*.'

With the completion of these steps in the practical application of conscious declarations, most of the questions that were asked about their nature and structure have been answered. There remain only such details as the length of time they might or should take, how long or short they should be, whether they need repetition, and if so, how frequently.

The answers are that it is all a matter of individual choice and completely flexible. They can be as short or long as the feelings or thoughts indicate, just so they arrive at a point of clear conviction. Since all declarations are accomplished completely in the mind of the declarer, whether for oneself or another, it is only you, the one declaring, that can know. It is only your knowing that achieves the result — you of yourself do nothing. You are the instrument of the law into which you declare. You do not have to feel any effort or strain. This is the symbolic meaning of the words of Jesus: 'My yoke is light — the Father in me doeth the work', indicating that we are not personally constrained to move the universe, that the intelligent power that created it will accomplish this for us.

Repetition is only necessary throughout the approach to conscious thinking in order to wear away the resistance of habitual thinking and conditioning, until such time as the principle is completely absorbed. There are many repetitious phrases used in the declarations, and these are strongly advised in order to bolster their impact on your own mind. The truth cannot be reiterated too frequently. It never becomes less true, but at certain times becomes more apparent. When the consciousness is ready, it hears for the first time what it has long heard with the ears alone. Insights may be ardently courted, but finally come unexpectedly, by 'surprise'.

As for a specific declaration for a specific purpose, its success is estimated by its result: declare until the result is a demonstrated outer reality, has moved from inner acceptance to visible and verifiable experience. You, of course, will by that time have moved on to other declarations more vital to your current development.

When you declare for others, you simply put their name to the declaration. We are all one in Mind, our given name but a form of individualizing identity. A person known as 'Jane', could in spirit as well be called 'God-as-Jane'. This is why it is possible to make a conscious declaration for others as if it were for yourself, for others are you, and you are others. As Sid Caesar once observed, 'Once you learn who "they" and "them" are, you don't blame anything on them, because "they" and "them" are you — no one else is in charge of you.'

Finally, whatever the approach, whatever the words used, a conscious declaration must always contain the essence of its objective — to assert the truth of any given condition with the authority of co-creator in the infinite creative process.

Turning to the power with which you are inseparably fused, you might consciously declare in this way:

> I live because life lives in me. I move because there is a universal energy flowing through me. I think because there is an infinite intelligence thinking through me. I exist because this infinite spirit seeks to individualize itself in me. I now recognize this, believe it and act on my belief. I now consciously accept my responsibility to be what I truly am, and live up to all that life seeks to be through me. There is a place in my mind that merges with the Mind of God and I now draw power and inspiration from it. The radiance of the presence of God envelops me. In this knowledge of oneness with God, everything in my life is constructive, life-giving, blessed and prospered. (And so it is.)

== 10 ==

ESTABLISHING THE QUALITY OF EXPERIENCE

> We can improve the nature and quality of our
> thought only by personal inquiry into our thinking.
> That is, only by thinking about our thinking. We
> will thus come to recognize the kinds of ideas and
> attitudes that produce a good effect when we apply
> them to the conduct of our lives.
>
> J. Kennedy Shultz

There is nothing so elusive and obscure to our conscious mind as the true nature of what we believe about ourselves. What we think of ourselves, the underlying estimate of our worth in relation not only to ourselves but to others, may lurk and simmer in our reactions almost or completely undetected, affecting everything we say, think, feel or do, and often making the tenor of our own lives incomprehensible to us.

It is difficult to follow Shakespeare's ever-telling observation, 'to thine own self be true, and it follows as the night the day thou canst not then be false to any man', when we do not have sufficient clues as to who 'thine own self' is.

We are largely mysterious to ourselves. We may understand and accept the basic principle of the existence of spirit, and be able to practise its accompanying techniques with trust, yet still remain in the dark about who we are in relation to who we think we are. We may not be able to evaluate that part of ourselves which preceded cognizance, was established in the unformed consciousness of our infancy. Or, perhaps the quality was there, but got lost along the way with the loss of our innocence.

Ralph Waldo Emerson based his entire philosophy on the premise that 'We are wiser than we know', and that if we stood steadfastly by what we know within our hearts, we would live lives of irreproachable value, giving us the strength of our convictions and the contentment that comes of pure intent and motive: 'nothing is at last sacred', he said, 'but the integrity of our own mind — absolve you to yourself, and you will have the suffrage of the world — speak your latent conviction, and it shall be universal sense.'

Unfortunately, for most of us this integrity may slip like sand through our fingers, its traces lost forever on the beach, never to be recorded.

How has this happened, and why? Emerson points to two or three main enemies that come by stealth to erode our natural understanding and sense of God. They are *conformity*, the human addiction to *consistency*, and the *worship* of dead institutions, doctrines and the genius of certain men above others.'

Many observations of Emerson's have become integral to the moral values of Western man. His thinking was explosive for his times (1803-82), and today sound a rigorous challenge. We have become accustomed to hypocrisy and to compromise. Our violence imbues us with the belief that we are innately violent, with only a thin veneer of civilization to keep us from abandoning the whole flimsy structure as an invention of religion to gain control of humanity through fear of hellish consequences, or the promise of heavenly reward.

The natural existence of a universal intelligence that can be called God has been overlaid by rival theologies, adherence to opposing forces of good and evil battling for supremacy. Some of us may unconsciously harbour old concepts of the 'devil' even when we scorn them, experiencing them only as uneasiness, guilt or self-suspicion. Others may mock the existence of a sly malignant force, yet indulge in superstitious rites. Devil-worship is still a force in current society. All these considerations may be having their effect on our thinking, on the kind of thoughts we do not invite but which thread themselves through our unconscious self-image.

Emerson believed that the beginning of the end of our inborn knowledge of right and wrong, our basic alliance with an all-ruling, all-bountiful creator, was the intrusion of the beliefs of others in ways that became too prevalent and overwhelming for the preservation of immunity. For instance, if every person or circumstance of your experience required that you conform to their tenets of morality, respectability, education, behaviour, even speech and manner, and imposed them unremittingly on your own natural vision, the chances are that you would ultimately conform. Without being aware of it, you would have become a second-hand thinker, a mouthpiece for all the pre-digested ideas of the particular society in which you lived.

This would entail the loss of true self-esteem, the substitution of fitting in so as to pass muster, win approval, impress others with your worth, while remaining yourself unconvinced. The ghost of some greater sense of worth may haunt you, but you can no longer put a name to it.

Emerson says that this conformity must be fought from the start, before it can gain entrance and sabotage you. 'Who so would be a man', he wrote, 'must be a *non-conformist* — self-reliance is its aversion — to believe your own thought, to believe that what is true for you in your private heart is true for all men — that...is genius.' He also said, and most of the world has echoed it: 'Nothing can bring you peace but yourself. Nothing can bring you peace but the triumph of principles'.

His second assertion was that we may relegate our originality to unimportance under the fire of the accusation that it is not 'consistent'. Because you made a statement of one persuasion yesterday or some time ago, you lost its power to convince by having changed it, by having had another thought take its place. Thus, you forfeit your fresh thought to retain the necessary consistency. This, Emerson maintains, can hold up growth and progress of our thinking as it takes its natural course of expansion.

Emerson says of this: 'A foolish consistency is the hobgoblin of little minds'. This does not mean we should hop from one idea to another, vacillate, arbitrarily contradict ourselves, but we should not force our thoughts into a particular form for the sake of proving we are 'consistent' and therefore sound. 'Let a man know his true worth, and keep things under his feet. Trust thyself,' he said.

As to 'dead' institutions and worship of so-called great traditions, Emerson contended that 'If you maintain a dead church, contribute to a dead Bible Society, vote with a great party — I have difficulty to detect the precise man you are...But do your thing, and I shall know you.'

How familiar the comment to 'do your thing' was to become for future generations! Today if we 'do our thing', the assumption is that we cannot go wrong, with ourselves or others.

Perhaps in a world so torn apart with human confusion and denial of the 'real virtue' that Emerson claimed is inherent in each one of us, it has become difficult to believe that 'We are wiser than we know' — perhaps easier to agree that 'Our faith comes in moments; our vice is habitual.' Yet more encouraging: 'there is a depth to those brief moments which constrains us to ascribe more reality to them than to all other experiences.'

In summary, it appears that only by examining our thinking, scrutinizing its contents with a new and sharper perspective, can we hope to uncover possible disparities in what we believe we think and what we think we believe. Bringing these to consciousness may serve to free us of blocks hitherto too deep-seated to recognize or deal with. We do not need to be saintly, or superior to others, but simply to know how we truly stand within ourselves. From that point we will be able to move forward with greater ease, even if it means confronting unwelcome weaknesses and defects of character. It is always possible that we may also run across some unexpected strengths and find that we can be objects of our own love and respect.

The suggestion made here, therefore, is that the *we* becomes *you* — and that you set yourself up as an imaginary *centre of self detection*. This can be started with a list of questions and answers. To those listed here, add your own, as many as will come to you on close reflection. Remind yourself that your thinking runs non-stop, like a tape recorder left on permanently, so that *every* thought you have is on it. If you were to play it back you would hear *all* of your thoughts from the most trivial to the most adamantly stated without pause or interruption, processed through your brain to remain there until erased by different tapes of thought.

Ask yourself questions like these:

ON THE DEBIT SIDE

How much of my thinking is judgemental (of others and myself), self-condemning, self-derogatory, petty-minded, prejudiced, hypercritical, malicious, cynical, prevaricating, revengeful, fearful of being exposed as a fraud, an imposter hoping to convince others of my worth, my lovability?

Further:

What is the chief emphasis of my thinking? How much time and attention is it taking up on the unpleasant possibilities in my life, the worry of what adverse events *could* take place? How often do I think — 'what if. . .' and 'suppose' something does not turn out as planned? How much negative experience does my thinking anticipate, prepare me to withstand or do battle with?

How many of my thoughs are gloomy, morbid, compulsive, obsessed with illness, despair, failure, loneliness or grief, not only for myself, but for the world?

What percentage of my thinking dwells on war, poverty, the long nightmare of mankind's brutality towards its kind, to the creatures of the earth, the devastation of the very planet it depends on? How much does my thinking centre on giving up, ending my life? What, in my thinking, prevents me from doing it? What are my thoughts on death, on what happens thereafter?

ON THE CREDIT SIDE

How much of my thinking is friendly, compassionate, forgiving, well-wishing, empathetic, inspired to generosity, to giving without necessarily getting, inspired, optimistic, cheerful, focused on creating harmony in relationships or work, meeting challenges, helping others, ways to share what I have, to show my appreciation of beauty, nature, the fact of being conscious and alive, grateful, thankful, glad, loving, joyous?

Further:

How many of my thoughts, how much of my thinking dwells on constructive ways and means of expressing my basic faith in the goodness of life, its purposefulness, its meaningfulness? How carefully do I dissolve ambivalence with surrender to the trust that the immense intelligence that created me to know itself in the particular is the truth about me, and everyone?

What percentage of my thinking dwells on the limitless possibilities for the future of mankind, imagines and visualizes a world of peace and brotherhood, where only the *quality* of thought holds rule, and the transition to higher stages of development is no longer called 'death' but increased life?

Comparing these two opposing assessments, what has been detected, turned up into the light of your awareness? You need to underscore both aspects, draw up a charge of comparison. Where do you find the contradictions, the imbalance, which side, Debit or Credit, weights the scales? Do you see where there is a 'tug of war' within your beliefs, how first one side might have the longer end of the rope, than the other, with neither side able to win? And might this not explain an impasse in your experience where you can neither turn back nor go forward, cease to create ailments of protest in your body nor heal them, to direct your experience nor stagnate in indecision?

The way out of this closed circle is in your self-disclosure. When you can say — 'Oh, I *see*. So that is what my thinking has been creating as my destiny! Well, at least now I can start to do something about it!'

I know now that to change my life — I must change my thinking. I must start to think in a brand-new way. I need to think about who and what I really am, what I really believe to be the truth about life and my part in it, and to bring all my thinking into one harmonious fusion. Too long have I wasted my power, squandered it in self-rejection and opposition. Now I take my thinking on with full responsibility and awareness — I think what I *want* to experience, and Spirit supports me in self-mastery, proves it to me, honours it in concrete manifestation in my daily life. I have only to say 'so be it' — and it is.

=== 11 ===

EXCEPTIONAL LIVING

The ultimate validation of belief is action.

Israel Goldstein

It is one thing to embrace a principle, absorb it and put it to conscious use in our experience; it is another to confront the price of entering into a minority against the mass beliefs of mankind. Accepting a minority position is the conclusive test of our conviction. Either we withstand the cost of going against the herd, of moving in an opposite direction to commonly maintained materialism. atheism, agnosticism, rigidly established religious concepts, or we are caught in a vulnerable ambivalence that will preclude the exceptional.

As a third option, if we are to accept the necessity of being exceptional because of what we have come to believe, then we are faced with giving up all identification with mass orthodoxy. We must daily increase allegiance to our own principle and all its implicit truth. We must defend ourselves with the force of quiet faith. We must treat mockery as 'water off a duck's back', counter attacks without debate or the attempt to convert, speak out when the opportunity seems indicated, when someone is becoming open or searching in our direction. However, we must keep silent when people are closed and only baiting our ideas to knock them down with their scepticism.

You should be prepared for heated opposition, to turn and stand up against the outraged who might call you blasphemous, to answer from the cool reason of your completely made up mind. You do not have to claim that you are right, but you do have to believe that you are, to *know* that you are, and to feel totally certain that what you know will at last prevail, though it takes as long as it has taken us to arrive where we are now.

'Yes, all right', you will have to say, 'if you think I am odd, naive, a foolish idealist with my head in the clouds, unable to deal with facts as they are, it may gall me, but it won't hurt me or drive me to a defence — for I understand your lack of understanding.

'This does not mean to say that I feel I am a know-it-all, that my form of belief pales all others to insignificance. I am simply standing behind what I believe, standing firm, never for a moment wavering because I am outnumbered, on the periphery of commonly accepted, if not commonly *believed*, concepts of life and living'.

As uncomfortable as it may feel to be disparaged or declassified by those who feel they are the standard bearers of common sense or 'proper' religion, the exceptional must remain just what it is — exceptional, beyond ordinary. Extreme challenge is the corollary of complete alignment with the exceptional. Yet there is no alternative — you have started 'up the down staircase'. You cannot start down it again, for once its principle is established in your consciousness, your belief will never let you.

There is only one recourse open to you: be wholeheartedly, unstintingly exceptional. Act as if you were deaf and blind to the opinions and beliefs of the multitude, no matter how numerically impressive. Switch off forever those 'wise' voices in your head, those teachers, aunts, uncles, family doctors, authoritative parents, clerics, sage friends, who may echo with the ring of truth against your unfamiliar way of thinking. They are no longer the guardians of truth you once thought them, their knowledgeability and wisdom now shows holes, weak spots, fallacies. You now know a far more accurate source of truth, and you need no other.

'Having done all — stand'. This biblical reference may newly mean accepting a sense of ex-communication from old friends, of being the 'outsider' in groups, or 'hearing a different drummer' — not alienated from worldly pursuits, not minimizing their enjoyment, but without vulnerability to them. To you, all current emphasis on the economy and world chaos is a substitute for spiritual nourishment. There really is no more effective and constructive way to be of value to others than that you yourself become spiritually nourished: happy and resolved you can do more for those in need of spiritual sustenance than if you, too, were 'under-fed'.

With all this in mind, you are now equipped for triumph over appearance, for the fortitude of spirit that cannot be swerved from its omnipotence.

J. Kennedy Shultz has observed: 'Wouldn't it be interesting if public opinion demanded that all who preached goodness be required to prove their goodness? That all who claimed to have a way be obliged to show how they were taking that way and where it had brought them from and where it had brought them to? It would be so refreshing if our leaders, especially our "spiritual" leaders, would set us a clear example before they levelled upon us a lofty challenge. This might well be the kind of thing that really would save the world.'

He is doubtlessly right, yet it is not your claim that you are more exceptional than you can prove. If this proof takes time — after all, it is a 'do-it-yourself' process — at least you will be in action, ever moving towards your goal of conscious control of your experience — of creating your own tomorrow.

Here are some guidelines towards thinking in a way that will help you to create the kind of tomorrow you *want*. They are not presented as a set structure for you to follow like a blueprint, but as a varied source of ideas which may lead you to your own personal approach.

Conscious Declarations for specific purposes, and more general *Insights and Statements*.

It is hoped that these will fortify and augment your objective of exceptional living and the conscious control of your experiences, and inspire you to the practice that ensures successful results.

For further clarification of the imaginary division between the three ways in which the Universal Spirit, or God, expresses itself — Self-knowing, Self-contemplating, Self-conscious mind; its creative medium or subconscious Law of correspondence; result or effect in body or form.

These charts should now help to define where each aspect of our thinking belongs, and make clearer the role of the creative process by which the initial formless substance of Mind or Spirit takes form, how the whole particularizes as the part. They require close attention, for often the division seems blurred or perhaps too distinct. They should illustrate that the 'word' *is* 'law' to its own manifestation.

=== 12 ===

CONSCIOUS
DECLARATIONS

In using the term *Conscious Declaration*, there is a risk of jargon, which seems to be inevitable in any specialist approach to a subject. It occurs in business as well as most professions, and is particularly apparent in unusual philosophies, often with an irritating effect that diminishes their power to convince.

It is, however, difficult if not impossible to avoid doing the same thing here without encroaching on other terms already employed for a similar purpose: for instance, 'Treatment', 'Self-Direction', 'Scientific Prayer', 'Spiritual Mind Healing' and undoubtedly many more variations of what amounts to giving conscious directives to the Law of the Subconscious mind.

Because the term is appropriate and says what it means, it is used here in the confidence that it will accomplish what it sets out to do — which is to give form and definitive strength to the basic principle it impels into response.

Conscious Declarations can be applied to any aspect of life, from the healing of physical ailments to the attainment of 'bliss'. The general approach is to resolve all forms of problems with the truth as we see and believe it. This is that, despite all appearances to the contrary, we are perfect, and simply need to remove all limitations from our experience of this perfection in every area of our lives.

Before moving into the actual procedure, a word of caution is required as to what *Conscious Declaration* is *not*. It is not a form of 'pep-talk', used to galvanize optimism. It is not a device for hypnotizing the subconscious mind into positive attitudes and expectations. It is not 'pop-psychology' to be packaged and fed to a sales force to increase its productivity and override the resistance of prospective clients. It is not the ingredient that spurs a sports player to victory. It is not the programme for success-over-odds, or to build a loser into a winner. Above all, it is not a fortress against extreme tribulation.

All positive thinking is beneficial, often invaluable as a bolster of morale and motivation. It can make the weak stronger, the unsure more confident, the fearful braver, the vacillating more determined, and for those reasons alone is preferable to the mental toll of negativity.

However, any superficial positivism without a spiritual dimension is ultimately fallible, unreliable, subject to collapse when overtaken by the shocks, griefs and failures implicit in transient human events. It is fine while it lasts, but like a house built on sand, its foundations are never sound — a shift of tide or wind and the entire structure falls.

Conscious thinking, which attempts to take control of life-experience, is *not* based on 'getting high' on optimism, but on the comprehension of the power and the Law that works for our good as we direct it, a power and Law which can be seen to support our trust, that never fails us — not because it chooses not to, but because of its nature it cannot.

For *Conscious Declaration*, and some of the infinite variety of ways in which it can be applied, it is suggested that you do not confine your declarations to those given here, but take them as examples to 'oil the wheels', to get into the mode of declaring for every purpose and contingency.

At first you are likely to find them difficult to do for yourself; they will feel unfamiliar and you may find the wording awkwardly new, particularly if you are oriented towards an orthodox view of a God outside yourself and now have to bring it within your own consciousness — see it not as 'up there' but in your own heart and mind. In fact, many of us have been long in accustoming ourselves to this 'inner' God, and sometimes it forms an unconscious block or resistance to our otherwise willing acceptance. Intellectually, it may all make absolute sense and logic, but somewhere deep inside us, there may be a residue of the desire to worship from afar, to go down on our knees and pray in the old way.

Pay no attention, keep on working with the new way of thinking: gradually it will feel more natural, gradually you will be unable to return to the old way, and if you do, you will view it with tolerance as a habit that at times gets the better of your real belief; it will no longer seriously influence you.

SPECIFIC DECLARATIONS

The greater the consciousness behind the word, the more power it will have. Just words without conviction have no

111

power, and just conviction without words will never stir up latent energy. There must be a combination of the two to make a complete statement.

Ernest Holmes

THE NEGATIVE CONDITION

Lack (of friends)
I am lonely. People don't seem to like me or want to be with me. I yearn for friends and companions, but am forced to spend most of my time alone.

I am basically very unsure of myself. People make me nervous and I'm afraid of their opinion of me. I try to impress them with my worth and have a good façade, but underneath I have no real conviction and cannot seem to find it, hard as I try.

THE CONSCIOUS DECLARATION

God is unified with God in all. This One is now drawing into my life all love and fellowship. I am one with all people, and all people are one with me. I know no strangers. I am a friend, and draw friendship to me by the law of attraction. I give friendship and therefore have friends. I am companionable and therefore experience companionship. I love my friends, and they love me. I give thanks for this — for it is so, right now and ever more.

Because I am made of Spirit, a personalized form of the one and only power in the universe, I depend on no one's opinion of me. I identify my human self with my divine Self, my real Self, and have the supreme confidence that needs no reassurance from any other person or situation. It fills me with quiet conviction that has no need to prove itself. Relaxed, in perfect accord with my true worth I am now in confidently conscious control of all my own experience. And so it is.

112

THE NEGATIVE CONDITION

Lack (of finances)

I have great difficulty in feeling financially secure. I am always worried about running out of money, of not being able to pay my bills, of not being able to support myself or my family. I somehow cannot believe in having plenty, or ever being really affluent.

THE CONSCIOUS DECLARATION

Spirit, of which I am an inextricable and inseparable part, knows nothing of limited supply. My limited concept is of my own creation, and I now knowingly and consciously remove the boundaries of my conditioned expectations that keep me from the acceptance of unlimited finances. I now declare, with the authority of my God self, that all I can conceive and embody is right now available to me. I am receptive to expanded financial supply, welcome it, gives thanks for it. I know that money is God in action, and circulates in my life as in all of God's life, without limit. And so it is.

Lack (of prosperity)

I do not feel prosperous even when I have no reason not to: I cannot give of myself, reach out to others as I should. I am wary and pinched in my thoughts, do not appreciate the richness of living. In fact I feel poor in consciousness rather than prosperous. My experience has no lustre or joy. I feel guilty about the suffering of innocent children and those sad, starving people I am not helping. How can I allow myself to be happy and 'prosperous' while there is

I now declare my oneness with the infinite, unbounded, unlimited richness of the creator of this glorious universe and all it contains, which includes me, as well as the untold billions of stars, suns and moons, the glories of a vast cosmos, of beauty beyond human words. Oh, it is truly joyous to be a part of its infinite prodigality, to share in it spiritually and materially. My mind and heart are filled with the grandeur of it, the dignity, the love of all life and living

THE NEGATIVE CONDITION

bestiality and torture and fighting and violence all over this supposedly wonderful planet?

Fear (of life)

I don't know exactly what I'm afraid of, but this nameless fear comes over me, most often in the night, like a foreboding chill. It makes my heart race. There is a sense of impending disaster about it. It gives me nightmares, sometimes so gruesome that I wake myself up screaming for help! No amount of talking to God or trying to keep the faith seem to make it go away. It is as though evil really does exist, despite all the good reasons it does not, and that there *is* a malignant side to life.

THE CONSCIOUS DECLARATION

that this perspective gives me. I see that I can be a valuable part of God's creation; to myself, to others, to the world, an emissary and distributor of God's prosperity, which moves out from me like a radiant light, making happiness, harmony and peace wherever it shines. I give thanks that I am both a user and source of this divine light. I am what it is — as me. My consciousness reflects it now and forever more. And so it is.

Fear is a belief that God can absent itself from the universe it has created and that this particular entity, me, is cut off unprotected, uncared for and alone in a vast, impersonal cosmos. I now declare that this is an untruth, an impossibility, that that which made me of itself can only and does love me. I have only to turn, consciously, to this loving spirit within me, and it will instantly turn to me. I convert the energy of faith, and peace fills my being. All fear departs forever. My dreams are positive and happy. I sleep in calm trust. I move through my experience with the sure knowledge that God's Law is my ever-present support. As I let go of fear,

THE NEGATIVE CONDITION	THE CONSCIOUS DECLARATION

and declare my faith, it gives me back the power of faith to direct and control my own destiny. And *this* is the truth. So be it.

Fear (of rejection)

It is a terrible feeling I've had since a child when playmates left me out of their games. I never feel included, or a real part of any group. At the office they seem to ignore me, seldom ask me to join in their confidences or socializing. I interpret everything that happens to me as a rejection, and anticipate the feeling with dread. When friends or neighbours have parties and I'm not invited, it is black agony. I don't let anyone see it or know it, and you can't tell by my manner or expression that I'm affected or even aware — but a façade, no matter how convincing does not help me with the pain.

There is only one Mind, one Creator, one Spirit, one Life, no inside, no outside, just Infinite Intelligence and what it expresses. It could not reject any part or form of itself, nor experience any such concept for it is all in all, perfect, Self-loving, Self-supporting, Self-encompassing. I declare, therefore, that any sense of rejection I feel is me rejecting myself and has no other meaning, reality or truth. I now banish it from my consciousness, and replace it with the self-acceptance and self-esteem that knows its inseparability from a loving creator. I am consciously at ease with my fellow beings and forever more a part of them. When the old situations seem to occur, their pain is only memory. I love myself, as I know God loves me. This is so.

Fear (of death)

The idea of dying, of no longer being 'me', of leaving people I love, or being unable to complete my goals, haunts my life, making me

Life cannot die. The idea is a contradiction in terms. What seems to die merely passes from one form to another; all forms, of every kind, come to

115

THE NEGATIVE CONDITION

THE CONSCIOUS DECLARATION

afraid of risks, and of accidents, and exaggerating every ailment, no matter how trivial, as threat of death. I fear being mugged, being drowned or caught up in any violence. I fear that when I go to sleep I might not wake up, and am almost permanently braced in stress. I avoid funerals and cemeteries and the entire subject of death, as if I could make it go away by not acknowledging its existence.

go, to return to the unformed whole of eternal life. Only the body stays, to return to the atoms of matter that composed it. I declare, therefore, that my fear of death is unfounded, is in reality my fear of not living fully while I have the magnificent opportunity to do so. Life does not like being lived half-heartedly, and exacts the penalty of fear. I now consciously abandon fear, and give myself to this joyous God-given journey, and live my life as if to live forever; for I now know that I will. *This* is the truth.

Ill health (minor)

I am always getting colds. Whenever they are going round, in the office or in my home, I always catch them. I am extremely susceptible. The children bring them home from school, someone in our village gets them started so they spread to everyone, and I never escape them if I sit in draughty trains or get soaked in the rain. I avoid people who sneeze — I am helpless before their infectious germs. *My* colds are usually bad ones, lasting up to three weeks, or more. My worst ones are probably in the

Since the perfect God-principle of Life could hardly know or experience a 'cold', it must be some form of human emotion translated into a specific expression, perhaps a need to weep, protest, escape responsibility, or react to hurt feelings. If this were not so, the whole of mankind would be succumbing to draughts and germs the whole time. I now discern that I catch the 'idea' of a cold, am conditioned to the idea of catching colds and so programme my subconscious law that it promptly responds with the

THE NEGATIVE CONDITION

summer when I get over-heated then chill off. Colds are a cross to bear, and it baffles me that they can put men on the moon yet find no cure for them!

Ill health (chronic)

The health of my heart is in the balance. It is said that almost every case of heart trouble can be traced to thoughts of strain, disappointment, shock, prolonged worry, anxiety, pressure of work, failure in love affairs, marriages, careers, fears of old age, and so on and on. Almost any chronic emotional state, in fact, that puts a burden on the hard-working pump that circulates the blood causes a lengthy list of life-threatening symptoms, including, of course, heart attacks and strokes. Of these, I live in dread. Doctors tell me that the will does not control the heartbeat, that it is a reflex dilation and contraction controlled by sympathetic nerve centres in the spine, a physical action not part of Mind. This adds fear and helplessness to my heart condition and I am forced to take medication.

THE CONSCIOUS DECLARATION

manifest experience. I deny any further necessity for this and now consciously direct the law to erase the very concept of colds from my experience. I have fewer and fewer colds and finally none at all. For this I am thankful and grateful and look forward to my new, perfect, cold-free health. So be it.

The body cannot run the Mind. It is the vehicle of Mind, the means by which Infinite Intelligence expresses and experiences itself, individualizes its wholeness. As the centre of pulsating Life, the heart is the creative connection between the Absolute and the Relative, a fusion of Creator and Creation. I now understand and 'see' that God is my heart, and my heart is God — in action. I therefore consciously release every belief that my body rules my heart, and in peace and loving trust align myself with the truth of my innate perfection. All my fears recede and my heart functions perfectly. Love speeds my healing. I give thanks.

117

THE NEGATIVE CONDITION	THE CONSCIOUS DECLARATION

Ill health ('incurable')

It is said that no one can help me now: I have a terminal illness called cancer, and the doctors have no hope for my recovery. I am angry that this should happen to me, cannot understand why it has, because I am not old and seemed in perfect health. I may not have very long to live and a lot of pain to endure before I die, both in my body and the agony of leaving loved ones behind. If God is 'good', why does he allow such injustice, inflict such suffering? I have prayed but without result. When it comes to something like 'cancer', all the healing God is supposed to do breaks down. If there is this exception, then how can one believe any of the rest about a 'loving and nurturing God'?

There is but one Mind and we are in it and of it. It cannot know, therefore cannot sustain, any false growth. There is no place it can be rooted, no valid law to nourish or feed it: and disease without thought could not manifest, no matter what the name is given to the disease. Accordingly, I now consciously declare that no matter how my thought caused or originated this false growth, it can no longer remain in my body, because my thoughts do not accept the reality. God-life in and through me, now forever cleanses, heals, and renews every organ, and every atom in my body, after its pattern of perfection. I now totally and forever eradicate from my consciousness all acceptance or any acknowledgement of the possible existence of 'cancer' or any other form of 'malignant' growth. I am free of the very concept. Every cell of my being expresses its perfect health. I accept this *is* so.

POSITIVE DECLARATIONS

For Today

Today is all there is: the past is memory; the future is anticipation; only the present is experience. Today is 'the eternal here and now' of life, of our existence, and therefore:

Today I live as though I had never lived before. I see everything with new eyes and a fresh inspiration. I am not a victim of yesterday's experience or tomorrow's promise. I live in the fullness of the now! I think about the creative potential within me. I accept my destiny as a forward movement of life.

The one reality expresses itself in me and my world of activity. I embrace this day of challenge with enthusiasm and joy. I expect the best, receive the best, give the best. My life is one of self-acceptance, self-appreciation, and self-expression. It is God made manifest by means of me — and I am glad and rejoice that it is so.

For Security

Life is the outpouring of Good from potential into experience. The one Life out of which all life evolves is the only infallible source of real and permanent security.

I know that whatever I set about to do has a good result. My spiritual security ensures the manifestation of all my needs and expectations. I plan my personal activities from a consciousness that knows Mind is always successfully completing the ideas I think into it. I am safe and secure in a spiritual universe that is governed by spiritual law. This Law unerringly increases, expands and fulfils all ideas impressed on it with the energy of love and absolute belief. Therefore in complete reliance I can trustingly accept greater ways of living, new avenues of expression, increases in supply and joyful relationships. All my experiences of good come from the security of a universal Mind that is complete in itself and knows only to give. In this assumption, I confidently live my life always, under all conditions or circumstances unshakably secure.

For this I am grateful, joyous and at peace.

For Success

Success does not mean the accumulation of wealth, the maintenance of position, or supremacy of power. Success means a life free from the burden of anxiety and liberated from the shadow of fear.

Therefore, I know that as I give I receive, and as I receive I give. There is an ever increasing abundance going out and coming into my experience, and new opportunities are ever opening up before me. I live in the very presence of expanding possibilities, and as I identify myself with the omnipotent Life principle within me that knows nothing but success, all the results of my desires and endeavours are made certain of successful outcome.

Always I am put in touch with the right people, with right ideas, and right action. There is no hurry and there is no delay. All conditions and events conspire, by the Law of Attraction, to reflect back to the sure acceptance of my success, in my relationships, the quality of my environment, in every aspect of my life experience. I accept success, expect success, unify with success. I am success. And so it is.

For Peace of Mind

When we become conscious of our existence as an idea in the Mind of God, we shall find that we are walking in pathways of peace; that something within us acts like a magnet to attract that which belongs to itself. This something is Love, the supreme impulsion of the universe.

I now declare, therefore, that at the centre of my being is Peace. In this Peace that holds me so gently I feel strength and protection from all fear, all anxiety. It is the Peace of God, and, underneath it all, I feel the Love of the Infinite Spirit of all life. I know that I have no existence apart from this Love. As I become more conscious of this Love, all lack, all doubt, all that is false slips away as the mists fade in the morning sunshine.

I am one with deep, abiding Peace. I know that all is well. I know that as I now permit this Peace to flow through my mind and heart, every problem is released. The way is made clear before me and it is filled with joy and harmony. Today I permit my mental house to be at peace. I know that my true home is in the loving source of my origin, and here I consciously abide. Peace is the loving atmosphere of my eternal home. My Mind is at rest, at peace, filled with the soft radiance of Self-realization and Oneness with Truth. And so it is.

For True Identity

There is the person we present to the world, the person we see ourselves to be — and there is the real person we seldom come to know. This real person is our identity with that which created us as part of itself. When this real self, or 'soul', becomes known to us, we are uplifted, inspired with recognition.

This, I now declare, is me. What you see at first is the physical me. There is more to me than first meets the eye. The truth of me is that I am an eternal part of the Divine Being. Part of the Master Plan am I. Created by ultimate, infinite Love. I am united at source with all that is.

Look closer and you will perceive my Soul. It is linked with your Soul too; and it is linked with the only Great Soul, the Over-Soul — the Infinite Spirit of Life. My soul reverberates and attracts like souls to it — my fellow companions, the words that come before my eyes — and the outwardly manifested experiences of my existence are here because I attracted them here. It is my soul that truly looks out at you, that truly loves you. Evolution is unfolding my insight upwards, to higher and higher vibrations of understanding of my soul, its relationship as part of the whole. Reaching loftier heights inwardly — my physical life also reflects greater happiness and fulfilment.

My perfect, beautiful soul is here for you to see — it is the real me. Know me and love me this way, as I know and love you by your divine nature also. The physical is but a trimming to the Beauty within. It is so.

For World Peace

The peace within us will extend to the world as each one of us is lighted with truth. One by one the lights will be lifted up, and merge, until the whole of human life will be enlightened and at peace. There is no faster or quicker way to make that day come than for each one of us to start now to find our own light and share it with the rest of the world.

I know there is but one Mind, which is the Mind of God, in which all people live and move and have their being.

I know there is a divine pattern for humanity and within this pattern there is infinite harmony and peace, cooperation, unity and mutual helpfulness.

I know that the mind of man, being one with the Mind of God, shall discover the method, the way and the means best fitted to permit the flow of divine Love between individuals and nations.

I know that, because the divine Mind has created us all, we are bound together in one infinite and perfect unity.

In bringing about world peace, I know that all people and all nations will remain individual, but unified for the common purpose of promoting peace, happiness, harmony and prosperity.

I know that deep within every person the divine pattern of perfect peace is already implanted.

Thus harmony, peace, cooperation, unity and mutual helpfulness will be experienced by all.

I know there shall be a free interchange of ideas, of cultures, of spiritual concepts, of ethics, of educational systems and scientific discoveries — for all good belongs to all alike.

I now declare that in each man and in leaders of thought everywhere this divine pattern moves into action and form, to the end that all nations and all people shall live together in peace, harmony, and prosperity forever.

And so it must be — and is — now.

SUMMARY

Having come to the end of the *Conscious Declarations*, it should be noted that they have been scant in personal specifications. In your own declarations, you would most often want to specialize the personal factor, fill in personal directives and details.

For instance, here is a list of subjects for Declaration that could present themselves in your daily life. In any that apply to you, go into all the aspects you can think of and incorporate them into your Declaration, *outline* them, step by step, but be sure of one thing — never try to figure out or imagine *how* the law will achieve or be able to demonstrate them. This is not your concern. Once you attempt to anticipate what seems to you the realistic practicalities — say of finding the right house in the right environment at the right price for you, when in the moment it appears an impossibility — you are placing a limitation on the law, imposing your own limited view on what, if left alone and trusted, it would effectively provide. Remind yourself that nothing is impossible to the infinite life principle and forget your own habit of 'looking at things practically' which means nothing more than getting out of your own way.

- Selling property
- Troublesome people
- Overwork
- Unemployment
- Marital discord
- Sexual problems
- Business difficulty
- Relationship conflict
- Extreme emergencies
- Resentment
- Bereavement
- A demanding interview
- A legal case
- Unwanted pregnancy
- Quarrels with children
- Desertion
- Giving birth
- The right partner
- Alcoholism
- Drug addiction
- 'Natural' disasters
- Tragic events
- Physical handicap

In these situations and an infinite variety besides, remind yourself that what you created as your experience before you were conscious that you did so, can and will be changed at the moment you *consciously* decide that it will be — and for the better. This is the Law.

Naturally, many more questions will still occur to you, ones that may loom large as possible contradictions, imperfect logic or flaws in the principle of conscious control of your own experience. However, in time, as comprehension develops and deepens, it will be seen that negative thinking can accrue to affect not only individuals, but whole nations and peoples, in ways that appear to be randomly biological or indifferently cosmological. It cannot be so — for if there is a grain of truth to any one element of a spiritually based whole, it must apply to all of it. It must be all, or nothing.

The work of the human mind is to discern the way in which the whole demonstrates itself, to grow into recognition of the law of cause and effect as it inexorably applies to every thought ever thought, whether of unconscious or Self-conscious origin. One day this recognition may be achieved and there will then be no where to lay the blame for any form of negative manifestation of life, mental or physical. Responsibility will be neither God's nor the elements, but ours alone, the concomitant result of our thinking.

INSIGHTS AND STATEMENTS

It is best not to read these all at once, but to refer to them when looking for confirmation of what you believe, or for a revaluation that might cast new light on your thinking.

If you have no one place to concentrate your love you are blessed by giving love to many, to all if you desire. It does not become diluted, but ever regenerated. The more we love, the more love is there with which to love.

In the presence of infinite Intelligence all anxieties and fears are swept away like cobwebs from a sun-filled garden. Constant, unremitting bargaining with the Power (must cease!)
State your desires and say 'Over to You, God.'

If, by 'God', we mean life-essence, and not something apart and outside ourselves — then we must be 'God' as us! What else could we be?

All time element is now removed from my acceptance of good. My Good is now! *Good past, good present, good to come.*

All help comes from God — even if it looks like the work of a doctor, psychiatrist, the change of scene or release of worry. These are the presence of God! These are the forms of the demonstration.

Spirit in you can't be wrong! Go with Spirit and you'll be a genius. We are all potential geniuses!

All that you strive for — is what you already have! And all you want to be — you already are!

When you depend only and entirely on me *(your Self) you are completely supported. Dependency on me alone, as the source of all, reflects as dependability of people and circumstances or conditions. First — the prototype, the equivalent in me — then the reflection into manifestation.*

My support system is my own state of mind. My support system is my God-conscious Self.

I now align myself with myself. I am on my own side. All that restrains, diminishes, is released — forever.

There is a wondrous place where God does all *the talking — and I* listen! *God says: 'You are merely me individualizing myself. When you move out of your way, I am you speaking my words.'*

I don't have to prove it to the world. I have to prove it to myself. It will then prove itself to the world.

In the transient we only see partial answers to everything. In the absolute, we see whole answers. We can act on them according to one or the other or both.

When we are in tune with Spirit, then transient life is fun and exciting. It cannot be either of these if it is not first in tune.

With God on my side, how can I fail? Only when I align myself with human level 'wisdom' am I fallible and ever in danger of failing.

Turn more and more and more within to find more and more without.

Insight first, outsight second.

Anything is possible. But nothing is arbitrary. Everything works as Law.

When I receive a 'Yes' from myself I receive a Yes in my experience. We are the only ones who say 'No'!

It is more important to be the right person than to find the right person.

Don't tell the law how — Tell it what. Spend the other 99 percent of your energy in grateful acceptance.

Solutions are waiting for you to find them.

Every time we lapse we are getting ready for a higher stage.

In religion and spiritual philosophy God is sought. In mystic experience God is found.

The close to impossible is still possible.

I don't have to grow and expand into my God Self. I choose to.

The greater the test, the greater the trust and faith needed. Listen long enough and the answer will be heard.

If you are not at ease with the idea of joy, deliberately induce it. It is a feeling always underlying every condition, no matter how seemingly dire. Condemned prisoners have felt it, the dying often know it, even the tortured escape within it — for it is the very essence of conscious life. Joy is the true nature of God, your heritage and your ever-present strength.

We must be careful not to elevate the negative to undue power by giving it our undue attention.

The inferior and unworthy trend of our thinking is our personal 'devil'. Lift up our thinking, and the devil is gone.

Do not be afraid of your negative thoughts: just know them for what they are — not the truth, just negative thoughts. Give them no 'house-room' in your consciousness and they will dissolve into what they really are — false ideas, false concepts, with no valid law to sustain them.

The best way to serve others is to be sure and strong in your own conviction. The happier you are, the more you have to give.

Every now and then 'spring-clean' your consciousness. Rid yourself of old, outmoded state of mind and thinking. Cleanse the basement, the main rooms, the attic of your mental house of all that is no longer currently productive. Update, modernize, keep only that which is still of value today, and you will have made room into which fresh, new experiences can come into your life.

Choice is not really choice until it is self-conscious choice: until then it is unconsciously ruled choice, from conditioned response. Choice, to be of benefit to your experience must be knowledgeably arrived at, consciously applied and declared.

Spirit can manifest only through trust.

You do not help others by trying to do their work in Mind for them, by making their decisions for them. You can lead people to their own Mind by what you are.

SUGGESTIONS

Add to these insights and statements some of your own. Be still, tune in, become consciously aware of the presence of your God-

127

Self, listen carefully. You will find that your Self will speak to your self.

Stop a moment, write down what you have silently heard, not as a voice but as an inward communication. The truth it contains will be felt by you. Use it to be guided into right action, right decisions, right aspirations.

This will keep you in personal relationship to the impersonal Law, eliminate distance and the illusion of separation. Practised regularly, it will give you the confidence of identification with the source of your ever-available power.

SOME RULES
Do Not

- Lean on other people
- Depend on them to solve your problems
- Pursue superficial goals
- Try to impress them with your worth
- Grit your teeth with will-power
- Plot and connive for advantages
- Battle and struggle with adverse circumstances
- Resist the good open to you
- Push and press and strain for materialistic gain
- Try to force and coerce the Law
- Cling to habits and prejudices
- Nag others to get your way
- Play games with people's feelings
- 'Play-act', dissemble sincerity
- Be an opportunist for questionable objectives
- Compete under the guise of co-operation
- Give gifts to buy affection
- Attempt to control others with your 'love'
- Try to possess others, run their lives, mind their business
- Tell others what they should or should not do
- Take advantage of children's vulnerability
- Resort to cynicism under pressure
- Try to convert the unwilling or sceptical to your way of thinking

(Add many, many more to these from your own 'temple of truth'.)

Do

- Trust in your belief
- Accept happiness
- Be aware of God's presence in every aspect of your daily life

- Seek to harmonize any 'out-of-step' experiences or relationships
- Think whom you might comfort, give to make happy
- Dwell consciously on the beauty of life, the majesty and prodigality of nature
- 'Bless' and forgive those who may seem to have betrayed you
- Allow your consciousness to soar, 'reach for the stars'
- Replace fear and anxiety with the conviction of your belief
- Cultivate your talents, believe in them as God's gift of individuality
- Do the best you can with every day of your life
- Be wholehearted in all with which you align yourself
- Love others, but not instead of yourself
- Love yourself, trust yourself
- Allow yourself to be joyous
- Expect and accept only the best in life
- Greet each day as a new beginning
- Be ever renewed by the renewing of your mind
- Go beyond believing to *knowing*

(Add to these from your intuition. You will find there are more positive 'do's' than you were previously aware of.)

== 14 ==

POTENTIAL UNLIMITED

It is exciting to come of age spiritually.

Gary Zukav

Beyond the boundaries of psychology, physics and metaphysics — beyond the preaching, the teaching, the moralizing, the proselityzing, the self-appointed elucidation on matters fundamental to truth and salvation — we arrive at a place where all roads converge, and the way ahead loses its distinction.

It is certain that no one road has the definitive light to illuminate the shadows of obscurity and ambiguity. Despite all the philosophical, analytical and mathematical genius, the miracles of applied technology, the ardours of religious faith, nothing here is singularly clear-cut and unequivocal.

The reason is no less daunting for being obvious: no one in the past or present has ever been able to tell us anything concrete about life itself. It has always been pure speculation. No one really *knows*. What we have sought so hard and long to know has, so far, escaped us.

What we have accumulated toward any proof-positive knowledge is no more than an intriguing array of part-principles, discoveries and clues. We see how the twin laws of conception and creation produce form (e.g the *idea* of a chair originates in mind before we make it into a visible piece of furniture on which to actually sit); how chemical compounds of the earth inter-react; how human beings are likely to behave; the 'miraculous' confluence of our brains and bodies, the revealed codes of DNA that designate the composition of our genes, the extensions of elementary forces such as electricity from spark to the propulsive energy of space travel.

In other areas of research, we have learned to meditate, so intensely as to charge ourselves up into states of ecstasy, sometimes even levitation, to convince ourselves we communicate with the discarnate or travel with angels in other universes and hierarchies, yet still remain 'grounded' as to the nature of the phenomenon of life itself.

A great mass of erudite volumes, research laboratories carry the torch of inquiry, but what, ultimately, have they turned up that is in any way conclusive?

Next to nothing.

However, next to nothing is not absolutely nothing. There is a chink. It is through this chink that conscious thinking slips like an errant beam of light — not by theory or assumption, but by a result that proves one thing at least: that thought takes effect as experience, and that if we use it with intention and conviction it makes a creative law of response available to us.

We are no more sure why this should be so than any other seeker after truth, but we are not looking for human corroboration for support. We see too clearly that there is an intelligence at work that speaks to our intelligence, that it manifestly runs the universe, knows exactly what it is doing at all times, and does it with what we can only call 'love', the terminology of infinite harmony and order, of intrinsic perfection.

What we know is known as an inner recognition, not built of outer but interior realization. Like the mystic experience of bliss that cannot be captured on a biofeedback machine or scientifically experimented with, that remains forever 'ineffable', it is experienced and known in a way that can never be argued or shaken by reason and 'logic'.

So what is open to us, without being impelled to answer all the unanswered questions, to fill in the 'gaps' of final enlightenment, is simply, to 'get on with it', to put our backs into what we *can* control and affect, what we *can* achieve and be. Considering the promise implicit in conscious self-responsibility, conscious self-remembering, conscious self-cognizance of conscious self-direction, the possibilities of fulfilment are boundless.

Not all at once, but assuredly in time, as dependence on the outer effects of already-thought thoughts passes into obsolete currency, along with pre-ordinated fate, the inwardly directed benefits of fresh, spiritually empowered thinking will spread to encompass the whole of humanity.

Never mind that this transformation of consciousness may seem at present to be the wishfulness of dreamers and Utopians — once begun, the tide of self-mastery will never be reversible. What *is* reversible are defunct habits of thought and belief, residues of compulsion, resentment, obsession, which can be arrested and reversed at any given moment by conscious acknowledgement and choice.

As individual members of the human race, each one of us will be in charge of our own destiny, and since only we ourselves will be the recipients of what we decree, we will be equally responsible for its values. In our self-benefiting lives there will be no motivation to take advantage, exploit or deprive others, when all we want is already ours and at hand. Each of us will already be able to command our own good, no other route will be necessary or desirable.

If it is possible to imagine a world where there is more than enough of everything to go round, because no one any longer needs to hoard, claim or possess any particular area of the globe, then we can stretch our imagination to a mutual respect for the globe itself — and, concomitantly, shared gratitude and love.

From formerly conflicting goals, from the belief that we have no personal means to right wrongs or secure what others have that we have not without stealing or warfare, then we will be able to understand and employ our new-born, conscious power to entrench ourselves in higher, more altruistic goals.

What would the world, the human race, be like then?

Undoubtedly, as the self-contemplating, creative initiator conceived it — no less, no more than its substantive perfection become manifest — if only, still, in part. What more to unfold, to know. . .?

Ultimately, gratefully, we do not know more than that we are here, alive, awake, conscious, and that the conscious choice of what we individually experience is ours right here and now. We are not forced to wait for pieces to complete a puzzle, provide an impetus, assist conviction. We do not need to draw from some other person compensation for our own inadequacies, demand revenge, defer our joy to some hypothetical event before we can move on.

Not only have we got the means to designate the kind of experience we want, but we can also consciously impel it into effect. Nor do we have to omit large issues, such as the kinship of all creatures 'great or small', the rights of animals and all that share our planet. We need never relegate to the outside of our declarative power those seemingly hopeless beings devoid of mind, of conscious control. There is always a conscious declaration to apply to them, for we are all in and of one Mind. If someone prefers a 'karmic' price to present change, we can still declare them finally acquitted.

Above all, our potential for immediate verification of our conscious declarations begins to show itself from the instant we make them. To our alerted awareness, they appear in prompt and 'literal' response, to the degree of conviction we have put into them. If we hit a tennis ball against a backboard, it comes right back to us. It does not hover or go off at a tangent; it returns, and with the same speed and force with which it was hit. (This analogy may have its defects, but it does approximate to the action of the subconscious law.) The demonstration of the most trivial-seeming command will soon escalate into those of greater ambition and range. We will begin to recognize that our self-directive power is First Cause to unconditional action.

This is our new beginning, our rebirth into co-creation rather than willpower, resignation, blind faith, the aridity of no belief, and that 'cold bed-fellow', meaninglessness. It may not make us recognizably better off to others, but it will certainly bring us a great sense of relief that there is something practical, immediate, that we can actually *do* about ourselves, and our lives — about what we shall experience from here on.

Thus we can claim that *conscious thinking* is not only our salvation but our triumph. If we have been lost, we have now found our way — and the potential of our way can have no limit. Assured of this, we can take heart and move forward into our new direction with new resolve, new expectation.

BIBLIOGRAPHY

PSYCHOLOGY

Berger, Merril and Segaler, Stephen, *Jung: the Wisdom of the Dream* (Shambhala, 1989).

Berman, Phillip, *The Courage of Conviction* (Ballantine, 1986).

Cade, C. Maxwell and Coxhead, Nona, *The Awakened Mind: Biofeedback and the Development of Higher States of Awareness* (Wildwood House, 1979; Element Books, 1989).

Campbell, Anthony, *Seven States of Consciousness* (Victor Gollancz, 1973).

Coxhead, Nona, *The Relevance of Bliss* (Wildwood House, 1985).

Coxhead, Nona, *Mindpower* (William Heinemann, 1976).

Dunbar, Flanders, *Mind and Body* (Random House, 1942).

Eskapa, Roy, *Bizarre Sex* (Grafton, 1989).

Ferguson, Marilyn, *The Aquarian Conspiracy* (J. P. Tarcher, 1980).

Gerber, Richard, *Vibrational Medicine* (Bear and Company, 1988).

Glasser, William, *Reality Therapy* (Harper and Row, 1965).

Grof, Stanislav, *Beyond the Brain* (State University of New York Press, 1985).

Grof, Stanislav (ed.), *Human Survival and Consciousness Evolution* (State University of New York Press, 1987).

Gross, Richard D., *Psychology* (Edward Arnold, 1987).

Harary, Keith and Targ, Russell, *The Mind Race* (Villard Books, 1984).

Hefferline, Ralph F., Goodman, Paul and Perls, Frederick, *Gestalt Therapy* (Souvenir Press, 1972).

Hirschberger, Johannes, *A Short History of Western Philosophy* (Lutterworth Press, 1976).

Isaacs, Alan and Uvarov, E. B., *Dictionary of Science* (Penguin, 1943).

James, William, *The Varieties of Religious Experience* (Collins, 1960).

Jantsch, Erich, *The Self-Organizing Universe* (Pergamon Press, 1982).

Koestler, Arthur, *The Art of Creation* (Hutchinson, 1964).

Kovach, Joseph K. and Murphy, Gardner, *Historical Introduction to Modern Psychology* (Routledge & Kegan Paul, 1928).

Lewis, Howard R. and Martha, E., *Psychomatics* (Viking Press, 1972).

Lloyd, Peter et al, *Introduction to Psychology* (Fontana, 1984).

Masson, Jeffrey, *Against Therapy* (Collins, 1989).

Meerloo, J., *Patterns of Panic* (International University Press, 1950).

Melton, George, R., *Beyond AIDS* (Brotherhead Press, 1988).

Merry, Tony, *A Guide to the Person Centred Approach* (The Association for Humanistic Psychology, 1962).

Miller, George A., *Psychology, the Science of Mental Life* (Hutchinson, 1964).

Muses, Charles and Young, Arthur M. (eds.), *Consciousness and Reality* (E.P. Dutton, 1972).

Needleman, Jacob, *The New Religions* (Allen Lane, 1972).

Pelletier, Kenneth R., *Mind as Healer, Mind as Slayer* (Delacote Press by arrangement with Robert Briggs Associates, 1977).

Ray, Marie Baynon, *Doctors of the Mind* (Little, Brown & Co., 1946).

Rogers, Carl, *Encounter Groups* (Penguin, 1969).

Russell, Peter, *The Awakening Earth* (Routledge & Kegan Paul, 1982).

Rycroft, Charles, *Critical Dictionary of Psychoanalysis* (Nelson, 1968).

Shaefer, Glen, *Universal Consciousness* (Translational Press, 1985).

Simeons, A.T.W., *Man's Presumptious Brain* (E.P. Dutton, 1962).

Temple, Robert, *Open to Suggestion* (Aquarian Press, 1989).

Thomas, Lewis, *The Lives of a Cell* (Bantam, 1975).

Underhill, Evelyn, *Mysticism* (Methuen, 1977).

Walsh, Roger, *Staying Alive* (Shambhala, 1984).

Warnock, Mary, *Memory* (Faber, 1987).

Weber, Rene, *Dialogues with Scientists and Sages* (Routledge & Kegan Paul, 1986).

White, John (ed.), *The Highest State of Consciousness,* (Doubleday, 1972).

White, John (ed.), *What is Enlightenment?* (The Aquarian Press, 1988).

Wilber, Ken, *The Atman Project* (Theosophical Publishing House (Quest), 1980).

Zukav, Gary, *The Seat of the Soul* (Simon & Schuster, 1990).

SCIENCE

Barrow, John D. and Tipler, Frank J., *The Anthropic Cosmological Principle* (Clarendon Press, 1986).

Bohm, David, *Wholeness and the Implicate Order* (Routledge & Kegan Paul, 1980).

Bucke, Richard, *Cosmic Consciousness* (E.P. Dutton, 1969).

Capra, Fritjof, *The Tao of Physics* (Wildwood House, 1975).

Chardin, Teilhard de, *The Phenomenon of Man* (Fontana, 1965).

Chopra, Deepak, *Quantum Healing* (Bantam, 1989).

Fromm, Erich, *The Art of Loving* (George Allen & Unwin, 1957).

Jeans, Sir James, *The Universe Around Us* (Cambridge University Press, 1930).

Joy, W. Brugh, *Joy's Way* (J.P. Tarcher, 1979).

Krishna, Gopi, *Kundalini in Time and Space* (Kundalini Research & Publication Trust, 1979).

Kaku, Michio and Trainer, Jennifer, *Beyond Einstein* (Macmillan, 1979).

Lilly, John C., *Simulations of Gods* (Bantam, 1976).

Polkinghorne, John, *Science and Creation* (SPCK, 1988).

Sagan, Carl, *The Cosmic Connection* (Doubleday, 1980).

Shaefer, Glen, *Universe with Man in Mind* (Translational Press, 1982).

Sheldrake, Rupert, *A New Science of Life,* (Anthony Blond, 1985).

Siegel, Bernie, *Love, Medicine & Miracles* (Harper & Row, 1986).

Stromberg, Gustav, *A Scientist's View of Man, Mind and the Universe* (Science of Mind Publications, 1986).

Uvarov, E.B. and Isaacs, Alan, *Dictionary of Science* (Penguin, 1943).

Watson, Lyall, *The Dreams of Dragons,* (William Morrow & Co., 1987).

Wilber, Ken (ed.), *The Holographic Paradigm and other Paradoxes* (Shambhala, 1982).

Wolf, Fred Alan, *Mind and the New Physics* (William Heinemann, 1985).

Young, Arthur M, *The Reflexive Universe* (Wildwood House, 1977).

Zukav, Gary, *The Dancing Wu Li Masters* (Rider, 1979).

SPIRIT

Andrews, Lewis, *To Thine Own Self Be True* (Doubleday, 1989).

Armor, Reginald C., *Ernest Holmes, The Man* (Science of Mind Publications, 1977).

Aurobindo, Sri, *The Supramental Manifestation upon Earth* (Sri Aurobindo Ashram Trust, Pondicherry, India, 1973).

Bailes, Frederick, *Hidden Power for Human Problems* (George Allen & Unwin, 1959).

Bailes, Frederick, *Your Mind Can Heal You,* (De Vorss & Co., 1941).

Barker, R.C. and Holmes, E., *Richer Living* (Science of Mind Publications, 1953).

Barker, R.C., *The Science of Successful Living* (De Vorss & Co., 1957).

Bass, V.W. (ed.), *Dimensions of Man's Spirit* (Science of Mind Publications, 1975).

Behrand, G., *Your Invisible Power* (De Vorss & Co., 1951).

Braden, C.S., *Spirits in Rebellion* (Southern Methodist University Press, 1963).

Butterworth, Eric, *Spiritual Economics* (Unity School of Christianity, 1983).

Curtis, D., *Science of Mind in Daily Living,* (Melvin Powers, Wiltshire Book Co., 1975).

Emerson, Ralph Waldo, *Essays* (Biblio Dist., 1980).

Fox, Emmet, *Alter Your Life* (Harper & Row, 1931).

Fox, Emmet, *Power Through Constructive Thinking* (Harper & Row, 1932).

Fromm, Eric, *You Shall Be As Gods* (Fawcett Premier Book Pub., 1966).

Gibran, Kahlil, *The Prophet* (William Heinemann, 1926).

Grayson, Stuart, *The Power of an Idea* (School of Creative Living, 1980).

Grayson, Stuart, *The Ten Demandments of Prosperity* (The Putnam Pub. Group, 1986).

Grey, Margot, *Return from Death* (Arkana, 1985).

Hardy, Alister, *The Spiritual Nature of Man* (Oxford University Press, 1979).

Hay, D., *Exploring Inner Space* (Penguin, 1982).

Holland, J.H., *Your Freedom To Be* (Hudson-Cohan Pub. Co, 1977).

Holmes, E., *The Science of Mind* (G.P. Putnams & Son, 1938).

Holmes, E., *Discover a Richer Life* (Science of Mind Publications, 1961).

Holmes, E., *Think Your Troubles Away* (Science of Mind Publications, 1963).

Holmes, E., *Creative Mind and Success,* (Dodd Mead & Co., 1957).

Holmes, Fenwicke, L., *Ernest Holmes — His Life* (Dodd Mead & Co., 1970).

Hornaday, William H.D., *Who Are You?* (De Vorss & Co., 1952).

Huxley, Aldous, *The Perennial Philosophy* (Chatto & Windus, 1946).

Johnson, Tom, *You Are Always Your Own Experience,* (Pathway of Woodland Hills, 1977).

Keller, Werner, *The Bible as History* (Hodder & Stoughton, 1965).

Kinnear, Willis, *The Creative Power of Mind* (Science of Mind Publications, 1957).

Kinnear, Willis (ed.), *Thought as Energy* (Science of Mind Publications, 1975).

Krishna, Gopi, *The Biological Basis of Religion and Genius* (Turnstone Books, 1971).

Kübler-Ross, E., *On Death and Dying* (Macmillan, 1970).

Lamber, Ruth, *A Passion for the Divine* (De Vorss & Co., 1979).

Murphy, Joseph, *Living without Strain* (De Vorss & Co., 1959).

Murphy, Joseph, *Nuclear Religion* (Joseph Murphy, 1961).

Nien Dorff, John S., *Listen to The Light* (Science of Mind Publications, 1980).

Ouspensky, P.D, *The Fourth Way* (Routledge & Kegan Paul, 1957).

Sangharakshita, Shaviva, *The Thousand-petalled Lotus* (William Heinemann, 1976).

Seabury, David, *Heaven, Hell and Happiness* (Science of Mind Publications, 1968).

Seale, Ervin, *Learn to Live* (Science of Mind Publications, 1955).

Seale, Ervin, *Ten Words that Will Change Your Life* (Science of Mind Publications, 1954).

Shultz, J. Kennedy, *A Legacy of Truth* (Brob House Books, 1987).

Skutch, Robert, *Journey Without Distance* (Celestial Arts, 1984).

Trine, Ralph Waldo, *In Tune with the Infinite* (Macmillan, 1970).

Troward, T., *Bible Mystery and Bible Meaning* (Dodd Mead & Co., 1913).

Troward, T., *Collected Essays* (De Vorss & Co., 1921).

Troward, T., *The Creative Process in the Individual* (Dodd Mead & Co., 1915).

Troward, T., *The Edinburgh and Doré Lectures on Mental Science* (De Vorss & Co., 1989).

Watts, Alan, *Cloud Hidden, Whereabouts Unknown* (Jonathan Cape, 1974).

JOURNALS AND MAGAZINES

UK Publications

Beyond Science (Nepturanian Publishing Co. Ltd.)
Creative Intelligence (Spiritual Regeneration Movement)
Kindred Spirits
New Humanity (Johan Henri: Quafer)
Revision (Heldref Publications)

USA Publications

Creative Thought (Religious Science International)
New Thought (International New Thought Alliance)
Psychotherapy: Purpose, Process, and Practice (Foundation for Inner Peace, 1976)
Science of Mind (Science of Mind Communications)

INDEX

THE SEARCH FOR THE BELOVED
JOURNEYS IN SACRED PSYCHOLOGY

Jean Houston

There is but one history, and that is the soul's - W.B. Yeats

All of us yearn for some kind of contact with the divine that will heal our wounds and give us a sense of oneness with the world and those who inhabit it. *The Search for the Beloved* brings the human spirit into contact with the realms of the divine and the Beloved of the soul through exercises, mythological journeys and rituals.

This extraordinary work explores the nature of spiritual yearning and shows how the reader may facilitate his or her own quest. It focuses on the four aspects of Sacred Psychology — the Great Wound, the Mythic Journey of Transformation, the Discovery of the Larger Story, and the Union with the Beloved of the soul. Following her pioneering *The Possible Human*, international author, scientist and philosopher Dr Jean Houston uses her magical style and warm insights to carry the reader's mind and spirit on a healing and transformative journey.

Never before has there been a book quite like this: a guide that describes the great known and unknowable homeland of the human spirit, an itinerary that leads the traveller to the sacred sites of the soul, a passport for those who yearn to bring their spirits into attunement with psychological depths and spiritual heights. More than a dissertation on the nature of the quest, it offers methods and techniques by which the reader's own search may be enhanced and the path made straighter.